Poems and Doodles

Poems and Doodles

Mark R. Smith

To order additional copies of this book, contact:
Xlibris Corporation
1-888-795-4274
www.Xlibris.com
Orders@Xlibris.com
124943

Table of Contents

A Word

A word to the would be wise,
don't worry.
A word to the would be strong,
don't fear.
A word to the would be kind,
don't hate.
A word to those who would love,
don't wait.
A word to the lonely,
do dare.
A word to the misfits,
don't fit.
A word to those who have it all,
don't sleep.
A word to the needy,
be greedy.

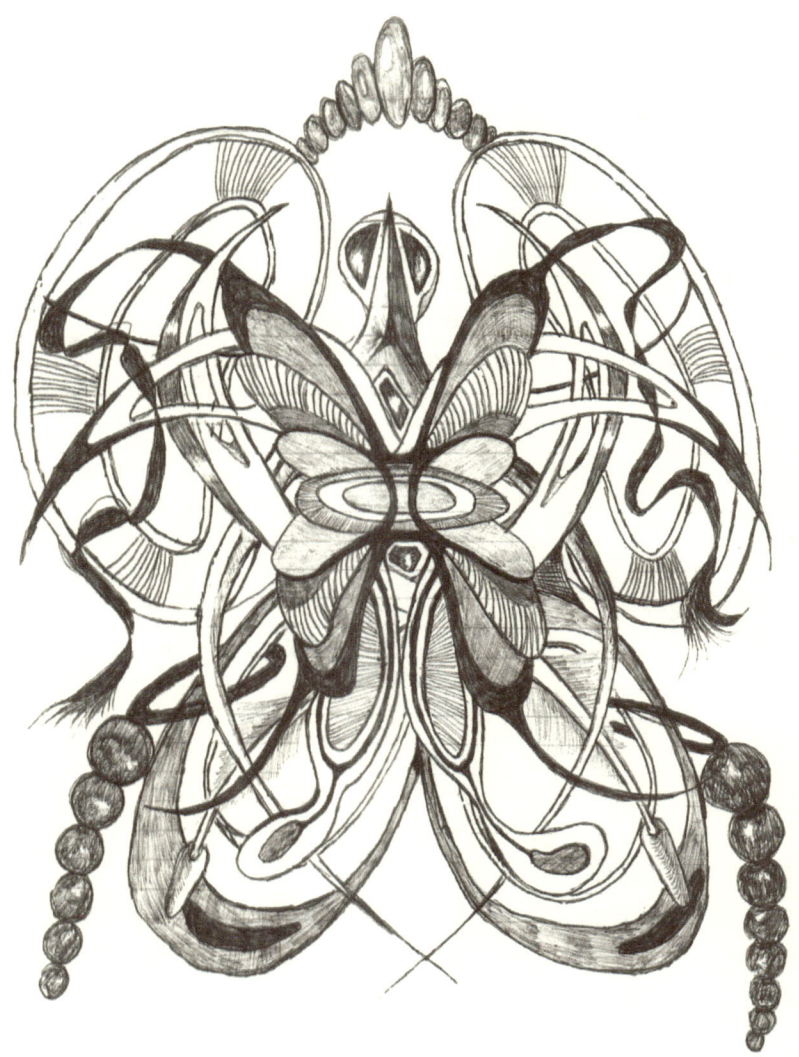

String Ship

Sea winds, solar winds, gravitational eddys, dimensional streams, the string ship will sail them all. Free yourself from old dirty sources of energy. The string ship is the ultimate in clean safe energy because it burns no fuel. Get your string ship today at a low, low price of $675 million.

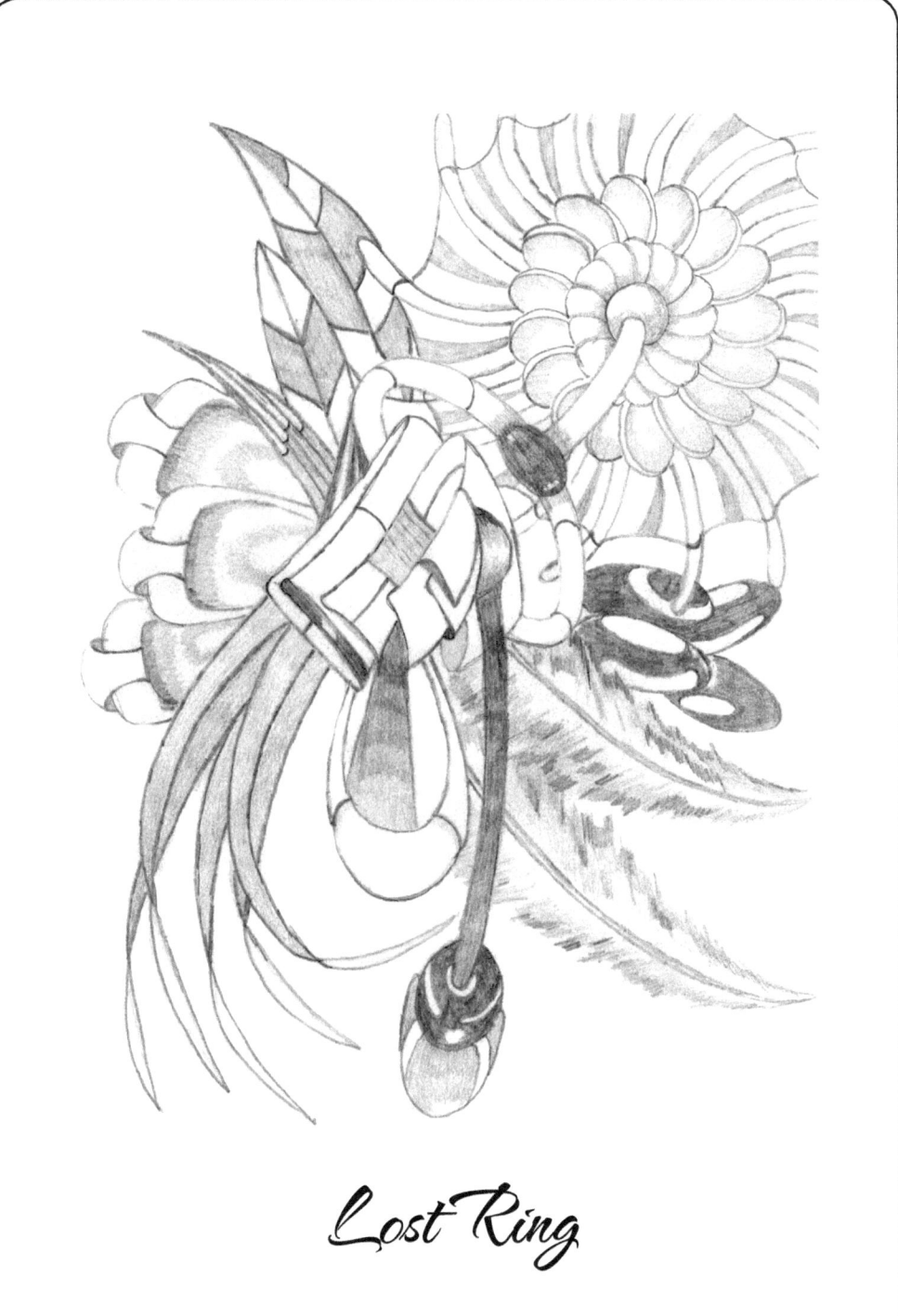

Lost Ring

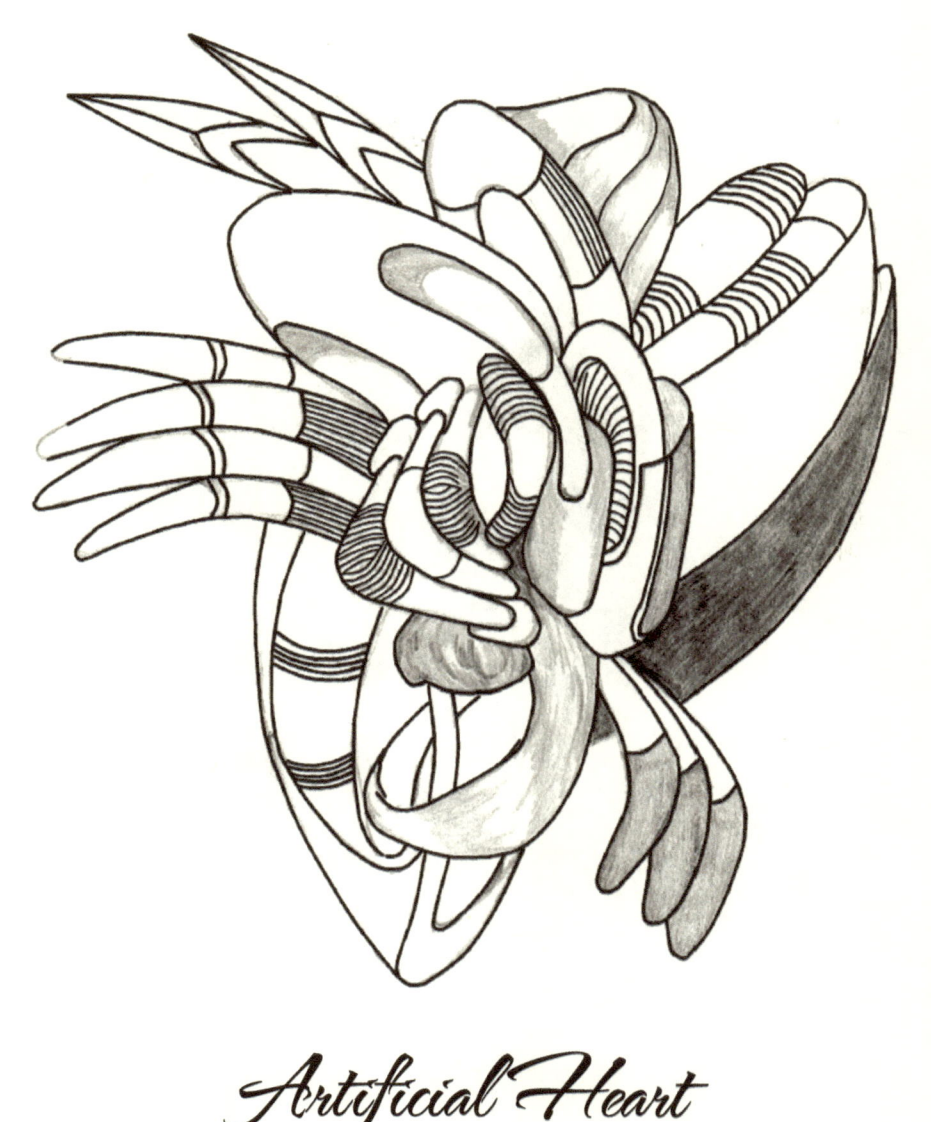

Artificial Heart

Broken beater, bum ticker? The AH-4004 will have you running marathons and climbing mountains in nothing flat. With the AH-4004 pumping you up, age will not be a barrier to super sex, super happiness or simply a super life. Makers of the AH-4004 cannot be held responsible for your failure to climb mountains and so forth.

City Sun

I can never get enough of the sun.
Somehow it always brings fun.
When things go wrong, on it I can always count.
Beating down hard on stone city streets, we play ball in the heat.
We challenge it to see who is stronger.
We use it to channel our hunger.
Drinks go down cooler.
Trouble becomes muter.
Smiles come easy and fast.
Don't worry about tomorrow.
Don't think about the past.
Pass the ball.
Hit the ball.
Throw the ball.
Run.
Sweat out what ills you in the pouring sun.

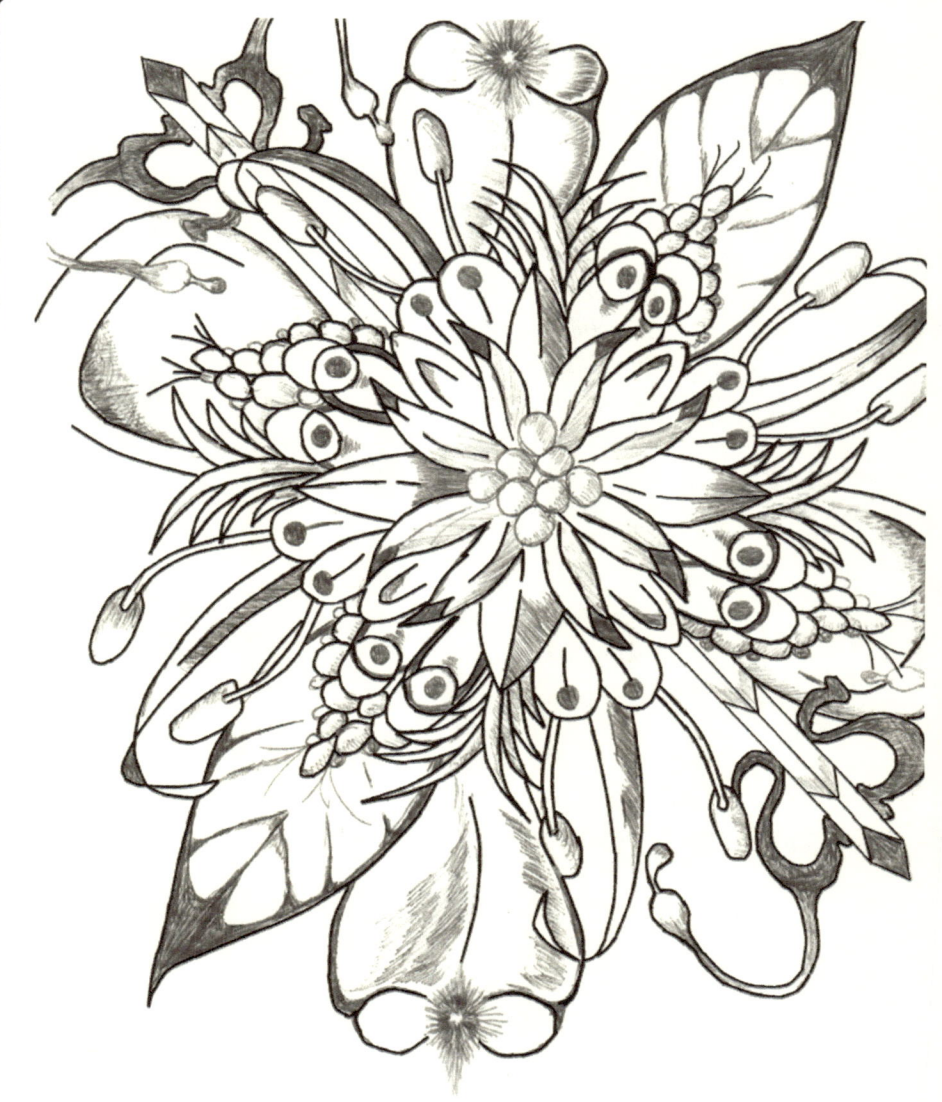

Stone Berry Flower

It's beauty is stunning. It's fragrances is devine. Hold it in your hand and it plays with your mind. Don't put me down you will hear it say. But hold it too long and the body will pay. Stone is not in this flower's name by accident. Stay away from it if you desire to see a new day.

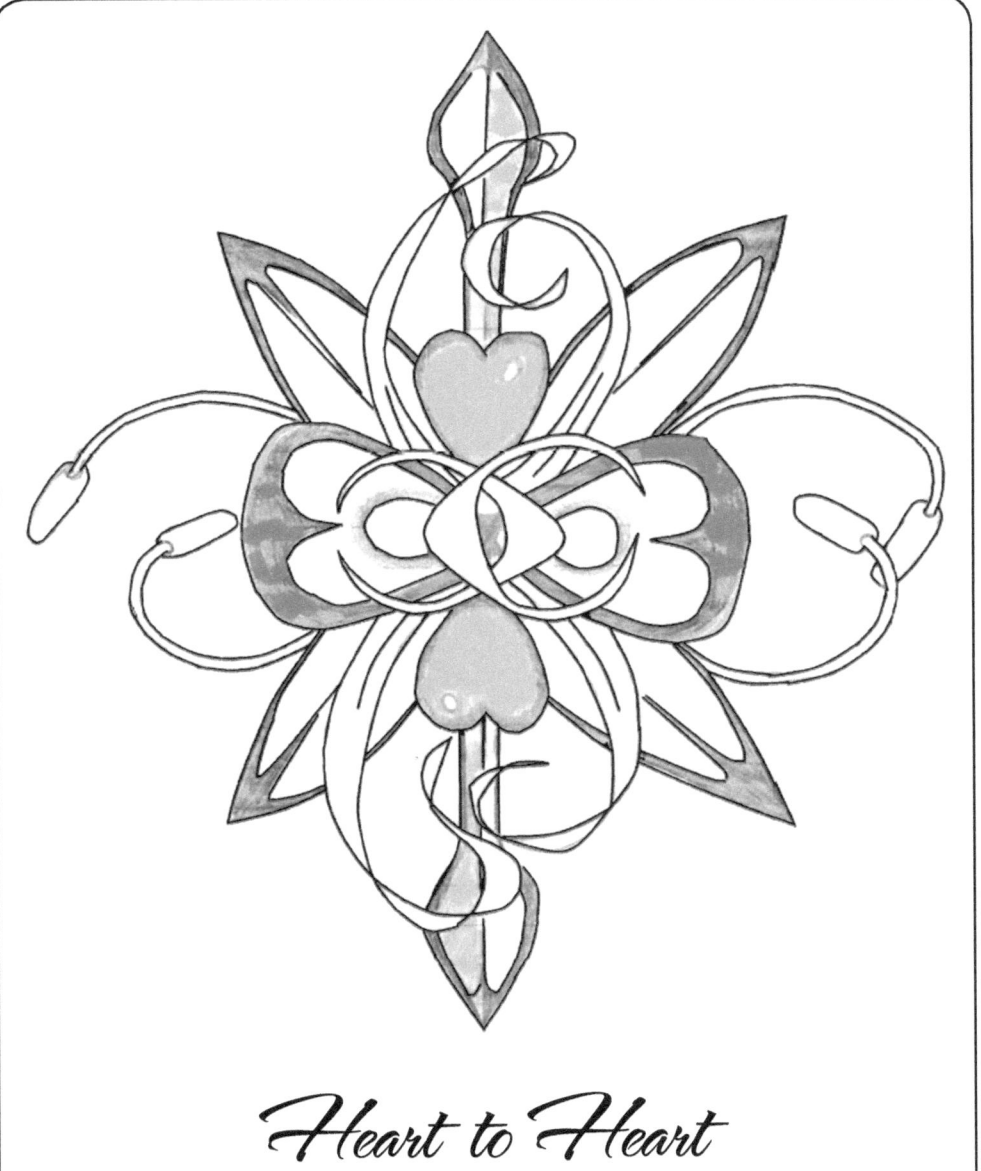

Heart to Heart

Two hearts beating, not as one. No matter how much someone loves me, they will never know me better than I know myself. No one can make me happy. Only I can do that. All someone else can do is provided an atmosphere where I can be happy if I want too. No, no one can make me happy. But they can make me sad. And the easiest way to do that is to believe they can make me happy.

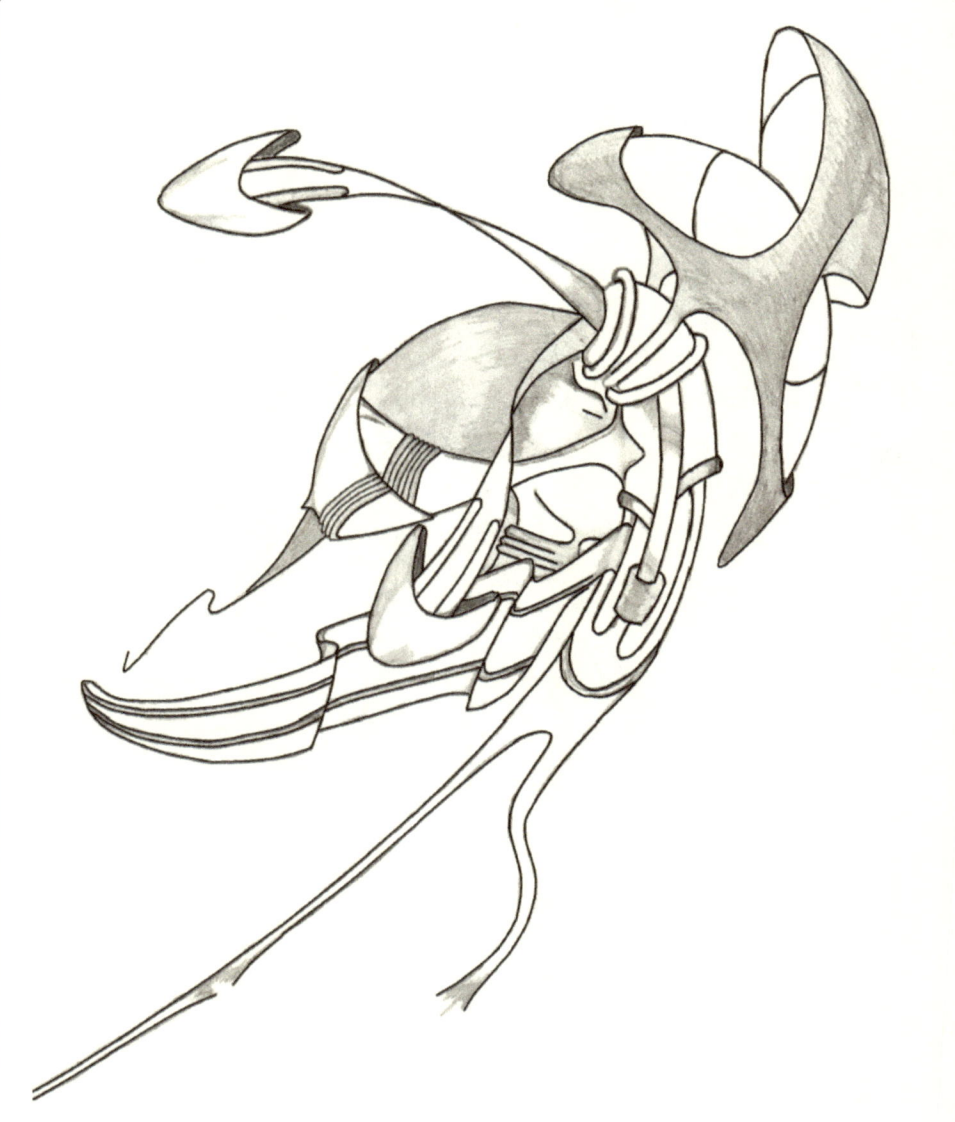

Robot Queen Abduction

She nor her subjects have ever harmed anyone. So their positive justification for taking her does not exist. Jealousy and pettiness are what motivates them. Or as my grandmother used to say, they don't want anybody to have nice things.

Desired Goal

To stay in the desired frame of mind is the goal.
Don't be swayed by negative souls.
Don't get steered down the wrong road.
Mental warfare, know of it, figure it out.
Be aware of it but discard its effects.
Down let it get you down, it is just a test.
No you don't have to let the dark side in.
It is just the devil looking for revenge.
He will threaten to tear you from limb from limb.
But you don't have to let the dark side in.
Nothing can penetrate your resolve.
If you don't let it in, it will just bounce off.
You need not react to others in a negative way.
If you are true to your heart, mean words, they just fade.
You don't have to let the dark side in.
It is just the devil looking for revenge.

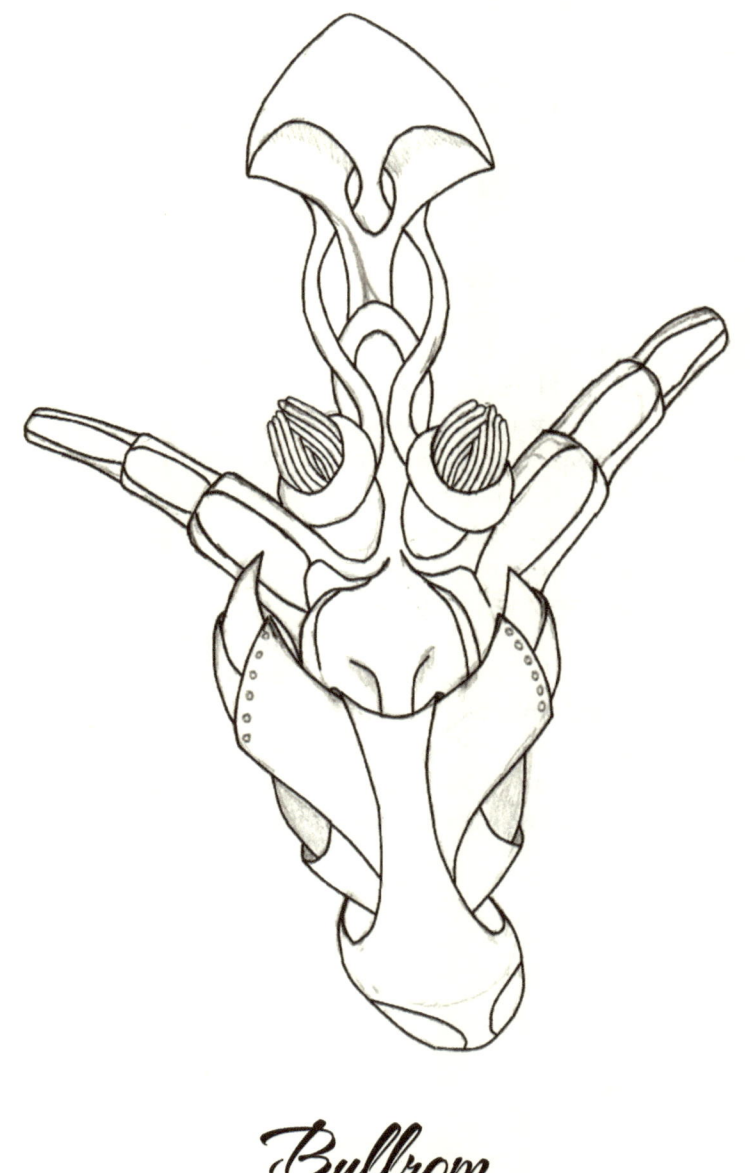

Bullrom

Sometimes what appears dangerous is only being manipulated from behind. To be really safe look for what is out of sight. At the very least, learn not to take everything at face value.

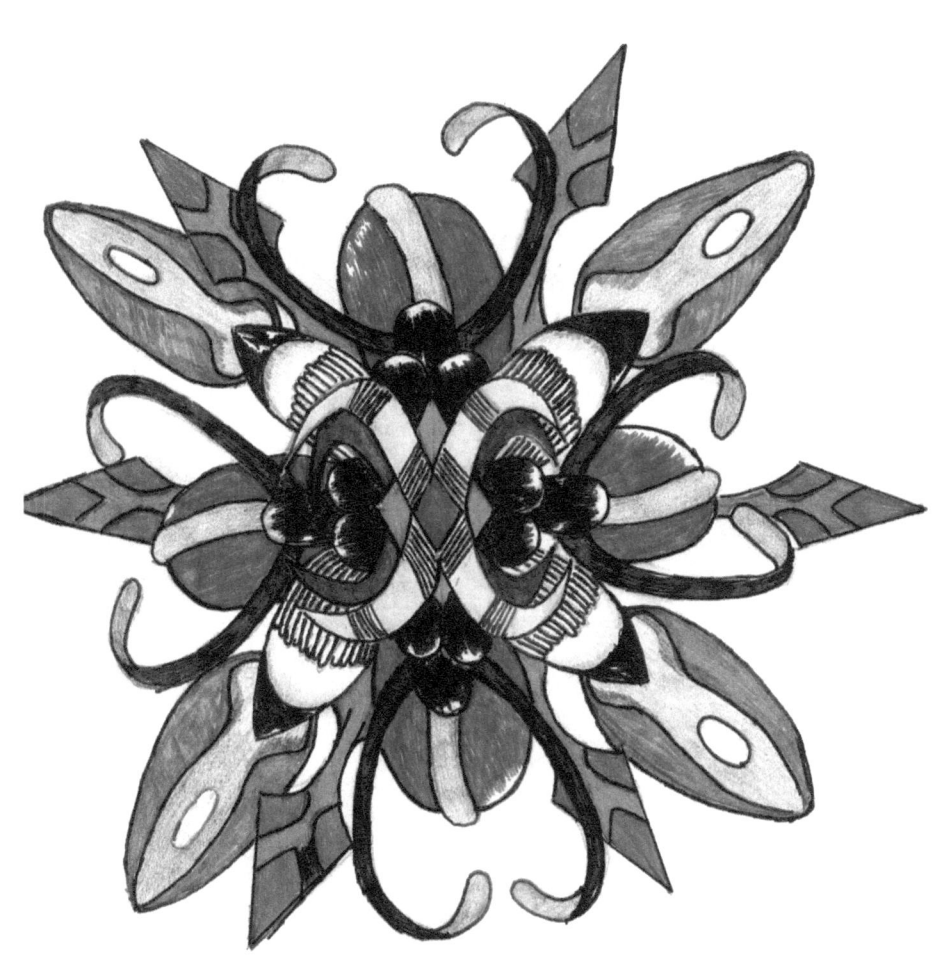

Cone Star

The cone star is significant of nothing in particular. It reminds me of royal symbols in general. If I had to choose something it represents, I would say it captures the self important, grandiose nature of the royal culture. After all if the royals don't believe they are important, no one else will either.

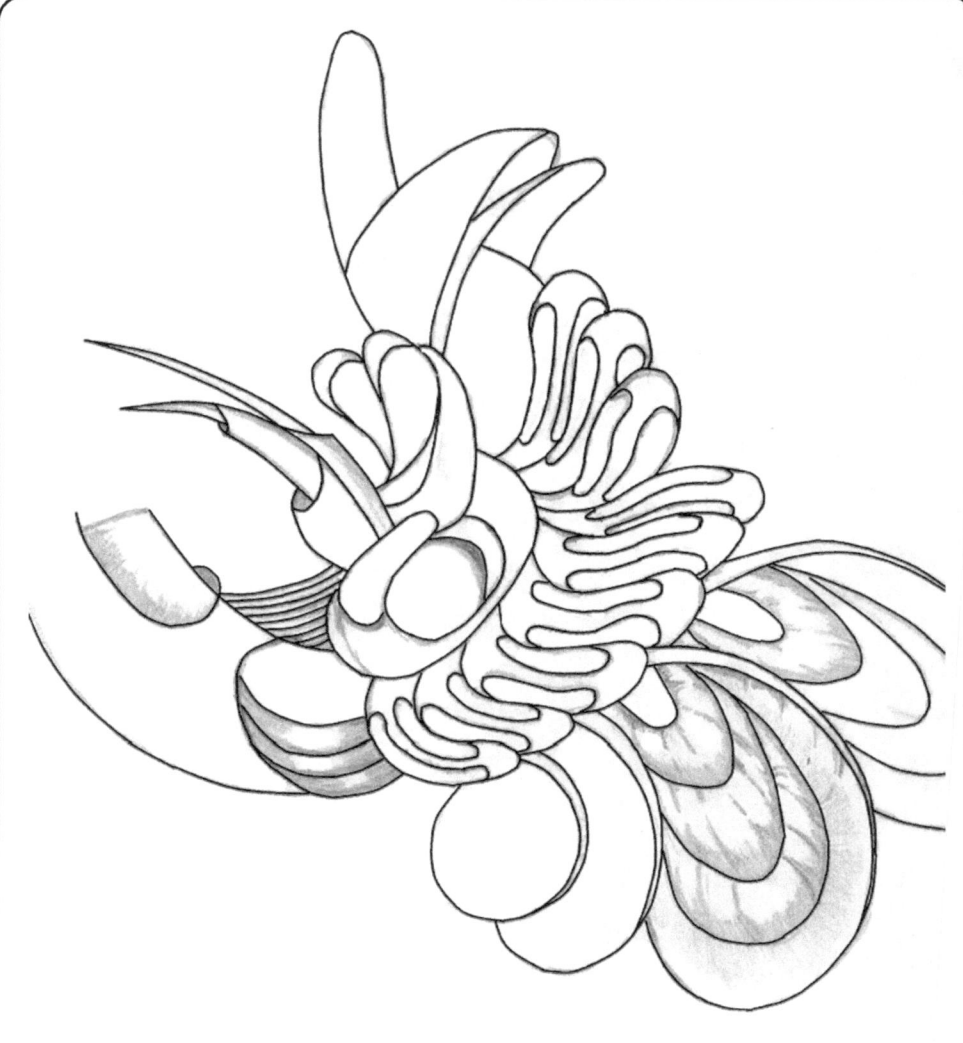

Mess

A mess can be organic or spontaneous. A mess can be ugly or pretty. Weeds in a forest are a basic part of nature. But in a garden they are the enemy. Like beauty a mess is in the eyes of the beholder. So if you know a messy person be tolerant. They have a role to play in life too.

Don't Worry

Don't worry about the day.
You know how to handle it.
You can do it on auto pilot.
Don't worry about the week.
The course has been charted so often in your mind.
Thinking about it is just a waste of time.
Don't worry about the month.
Think about the good instead of the bad,
And it will be time spent instead of time served.
Don't worry about the year.
You have already tackled the month the week and the day.

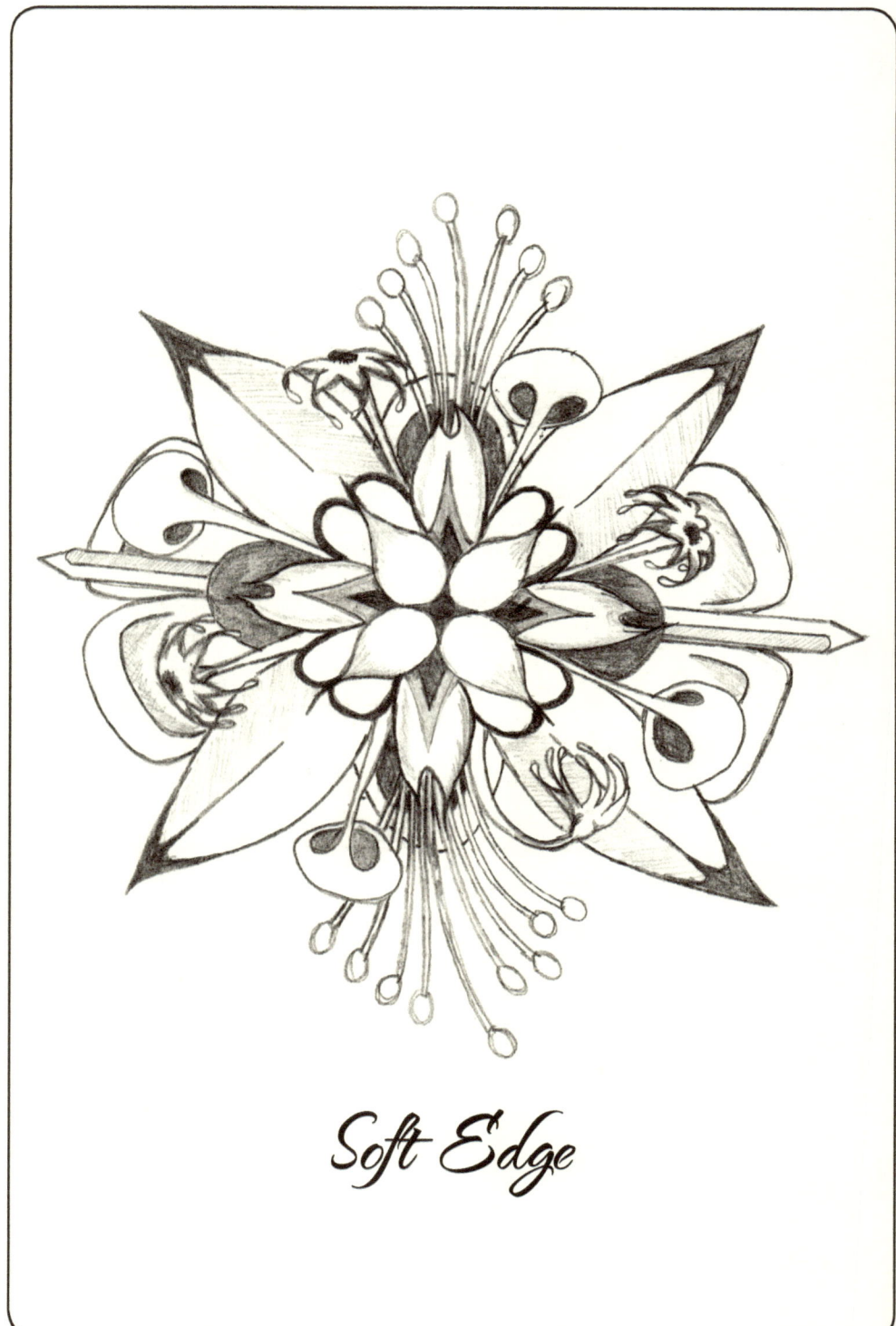

Soft Edge

Pretty Mouth

Don't worry, it is not evil. It is just hungry. You can feed it. It won't strike. There is no adventure without chance. Go ahead, feed it. It is just a little bitty old plant.

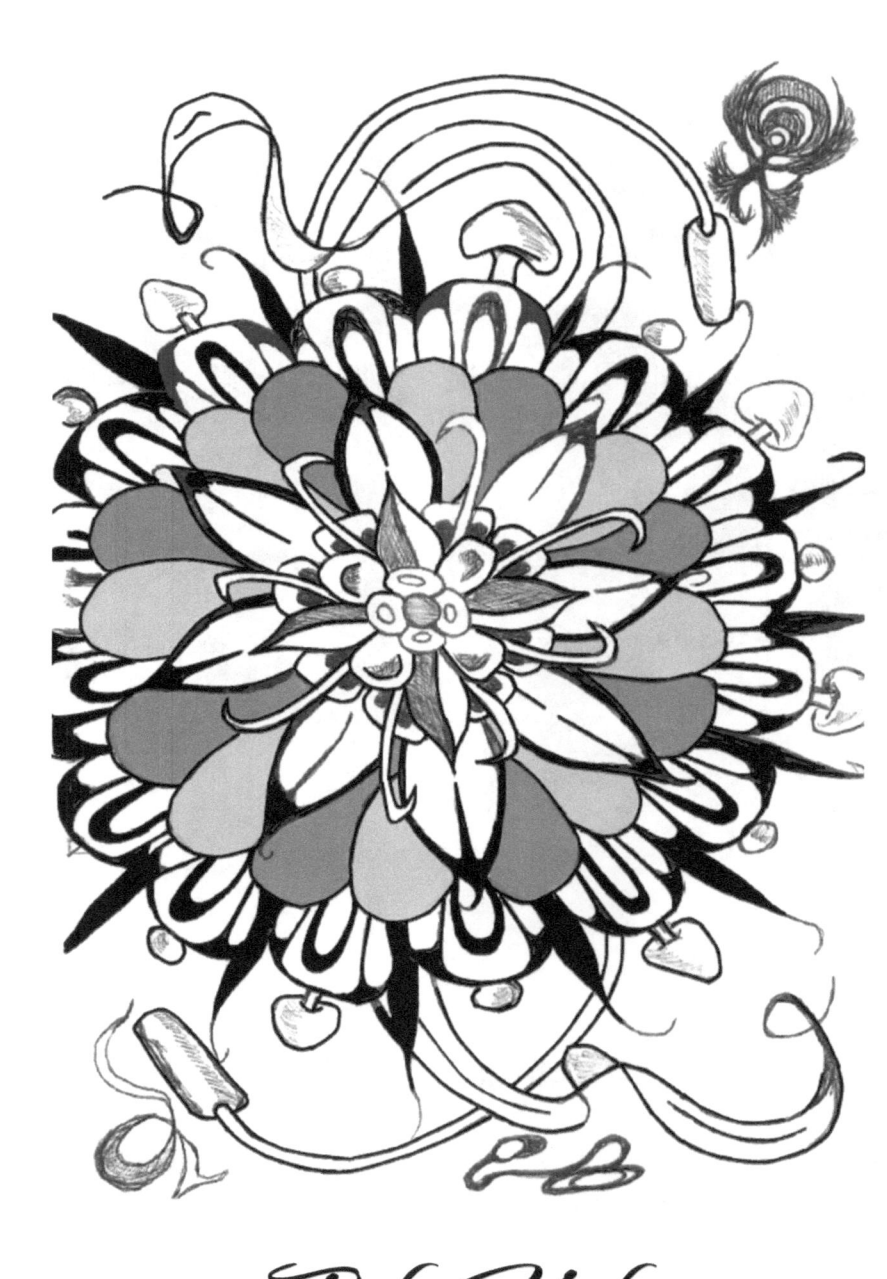

Tender Hooks

<u>Dumped</u>

Hearing you didn't love me, was rough.
Knowing you never cared, is tough.
Pulling my life out of the fire is Hard.
The emotional scars you left are large.
But to put that behind me I strive.
For real love I hope to find.
Infatuation will not do.
I only want what is true.
Finding the right lady won't be easy.
The wrong one I might spend time pleasing.
And as for you, I hope your next prospect does not raise your ire.
For no more hearts need be thrown on the fire.

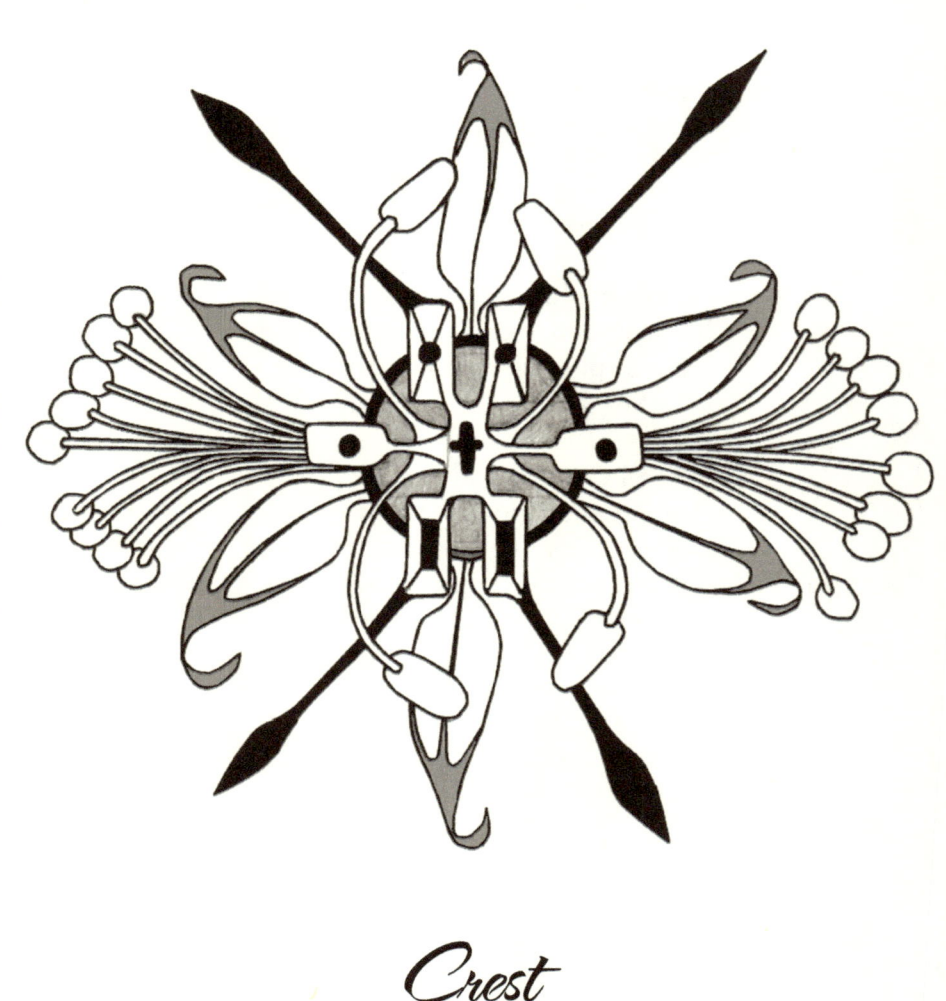

Crest

Who needs a crest theses day? They are old school and obsolete right? They are perceived as pretentious and pompous to boot. But in this age of fractured families and sky high divorce rates, having something like a crest to rally around don't seem so bad to me. Maybe it is time to bring back the family crest. At the very least, it won't make things any worse.

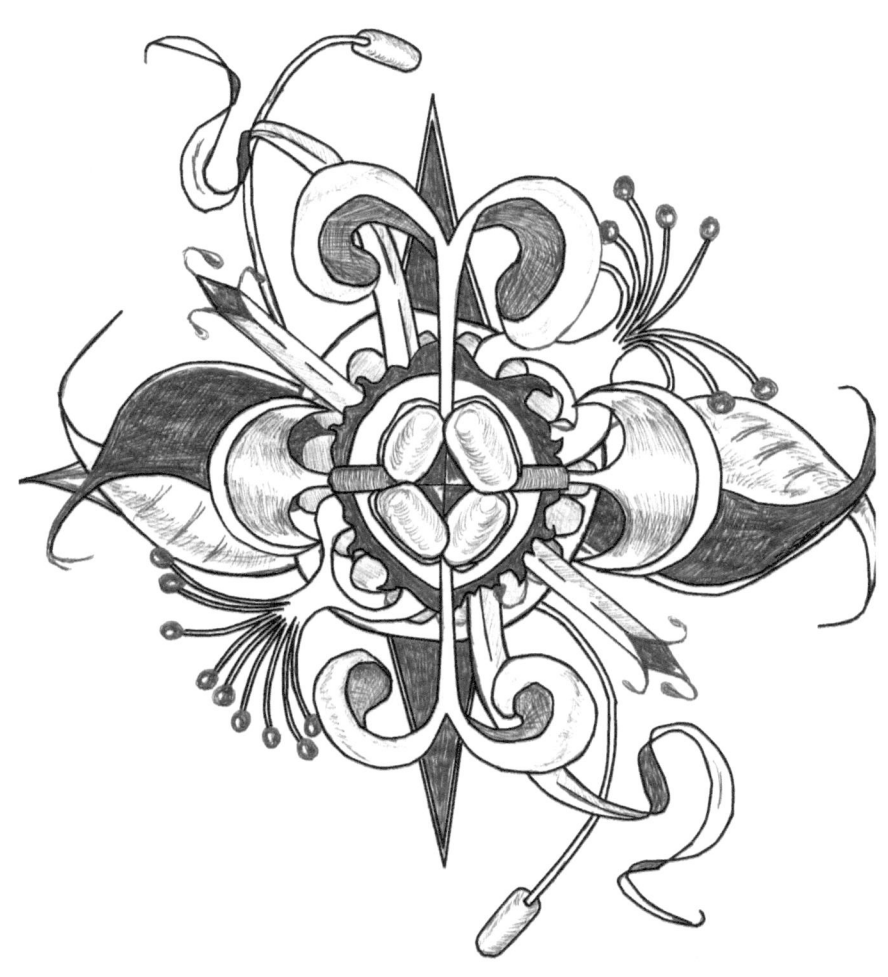

Center Burst

When the flower and blade cohabitate, all is well if the blance is equal. But sometimes the blade is dominant and evil is born. It is well known that evil is deceptive. This is why it is often beautiful. Fool the eye, fool the mind. Fool the mind and wisdom is blind.

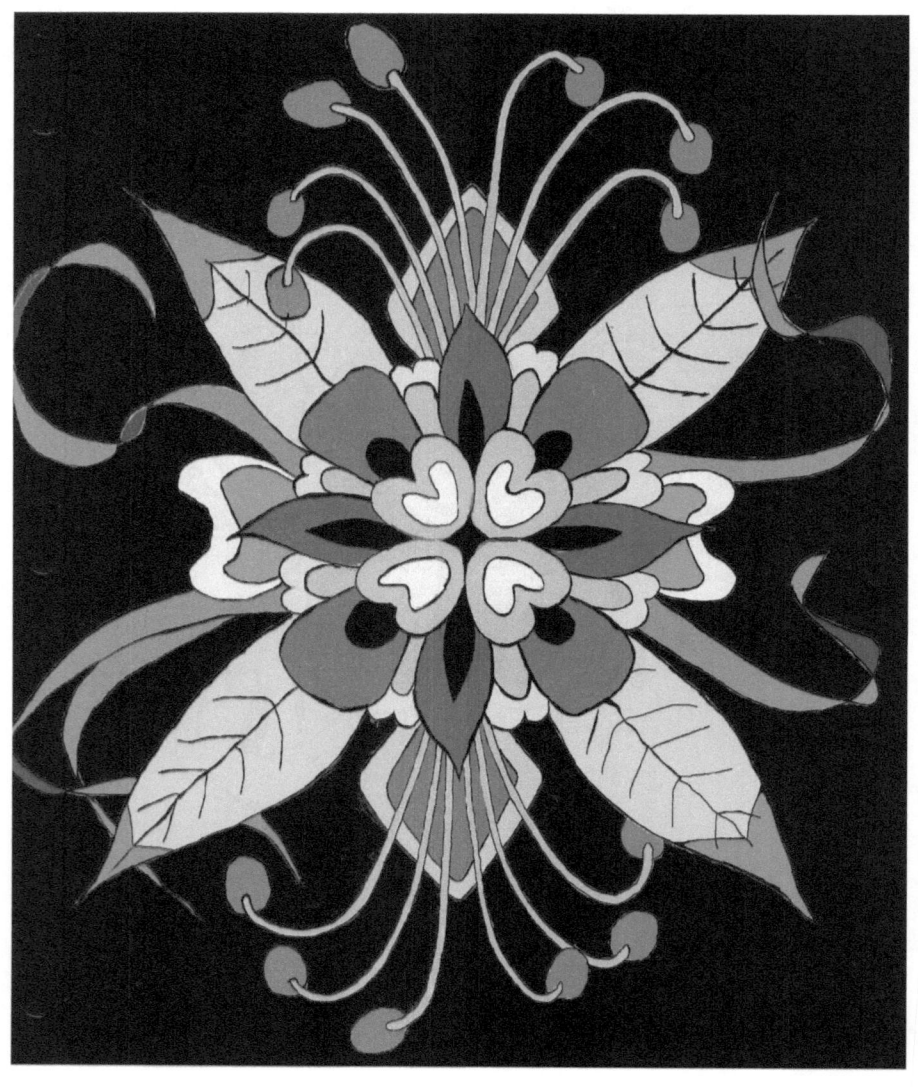

Candy Hearts

Endure

Stand it, persist, it matters little the ache of life at your center.
Care not does the mass that is the cause.
It affects them not, least that they are told.
Too dull, too worn are chosen thinkers to see the truth.
Life is a circle that comes around to me and to you.
One cannot be affected without the whole being influenced.
The sooner this truth is grasped the better the whole, the better the one.
But little hope is contributed to this event.
Too dull, too worn are the wills to make it haven sent.
Dog days roll on, accepted as the norm.
It is amazing what the soul will endure in order to see the sun.

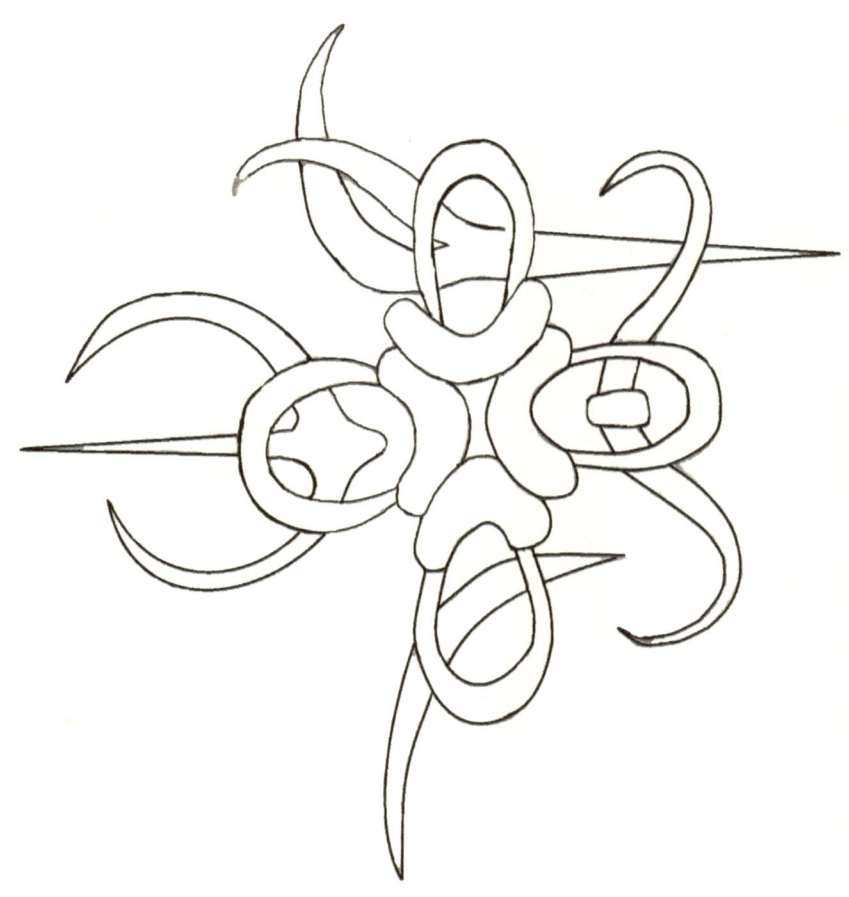

Needle Square

Everything in life is connected. Remove one piece and everything changes. That in and of itself is not necessarily bad. But tampering with a piece is a fifty fifty proposition. Because you can't see the end results until after the fact. And the change caused may be permanent.

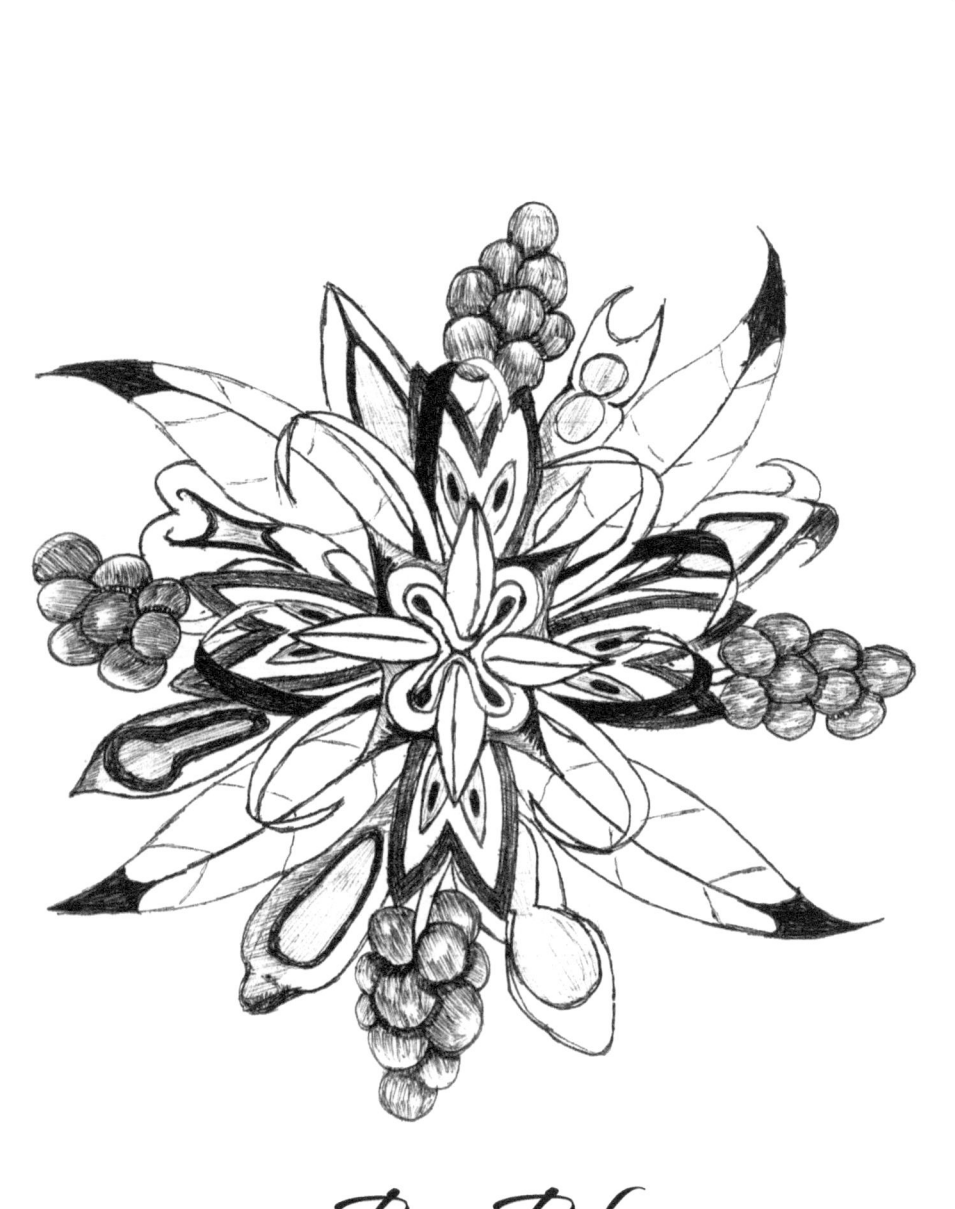

Bean Pods

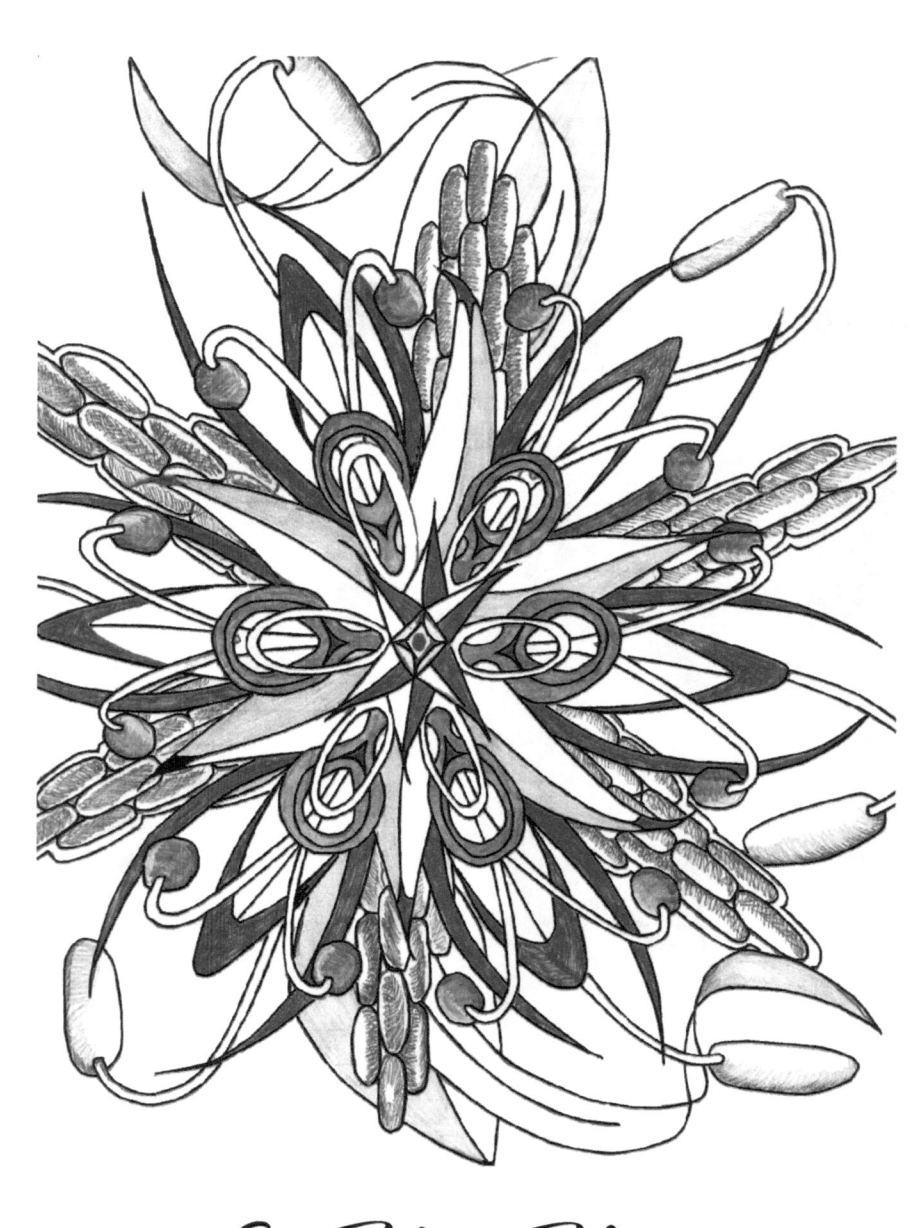

Six Hoop Flower

<u>Fear</u>

Fear is not to be feared.
Fear helps us accomplish things.
Fear is like a flashlight beam.
Fear is positive and spurs us into action.
Fear is a friend, without retraction.
It warns us when danger is near.
Move towards fear and your path becomes clear.
You will endure if fear you embrace.
Fear is an ally both vigilant and great.
Use fear has a catalyst to change your fate.
Without fear there would be no human race.

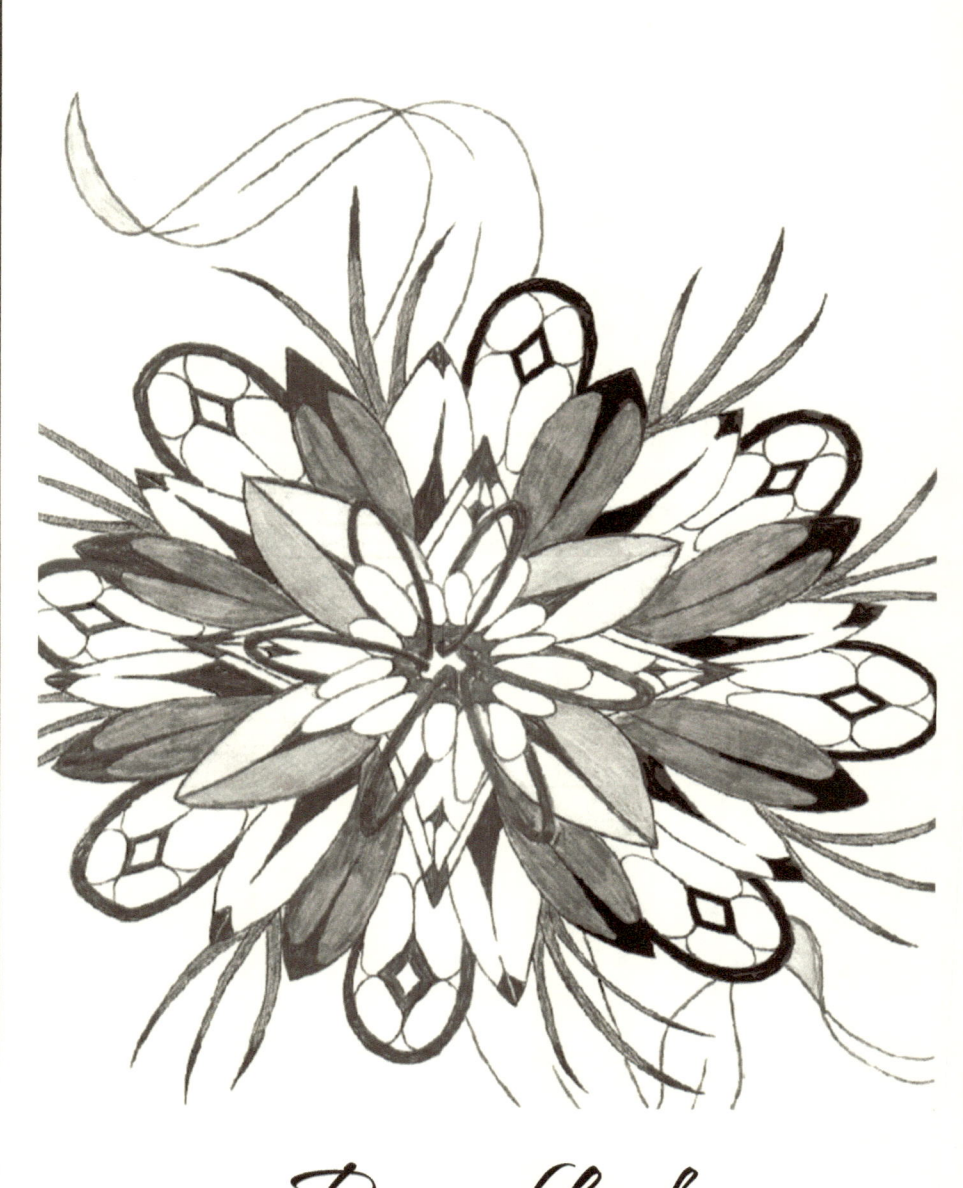

Diamond Leaf

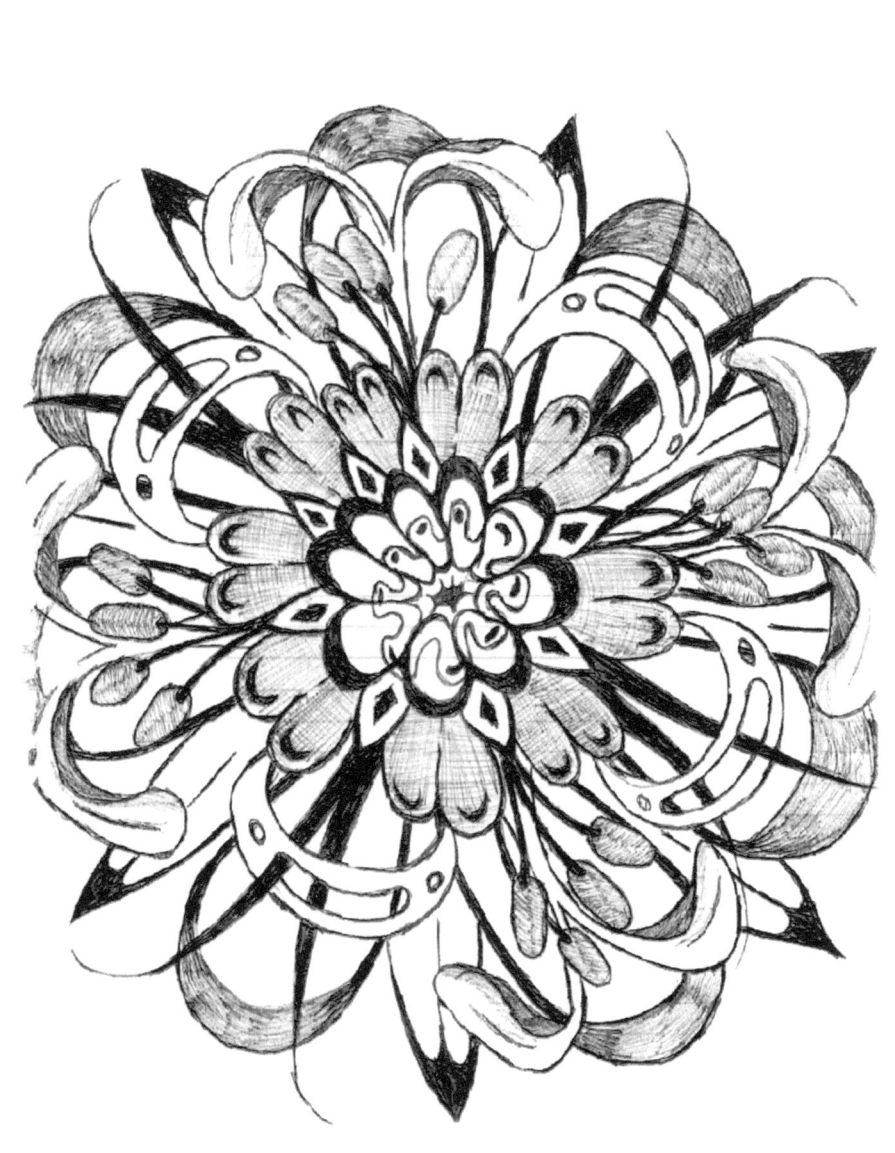

Rabbit Ears

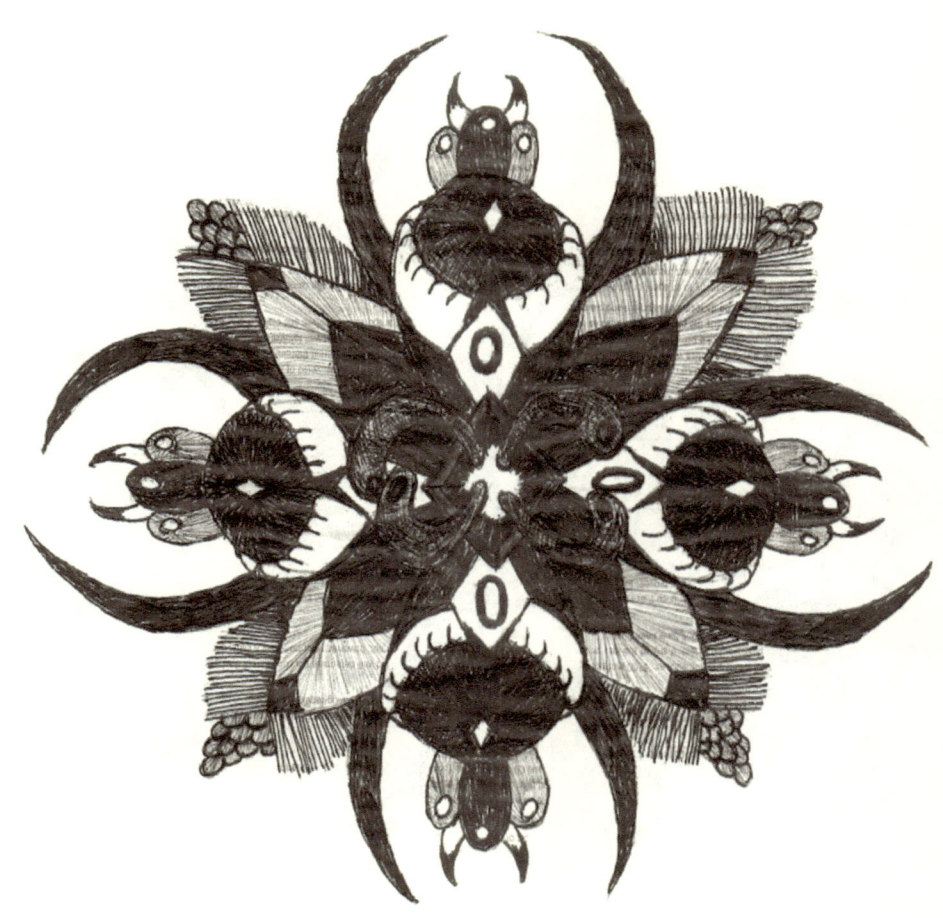

Spider Flower

Strange things emerging from what appears normal will startle if not outright frighten us. For those of us already mentally scarred, phobias may then abound. For those of us whom have been parented well, the event will merely provide a challenge to be overcome and learned from. Because a solution is always present, rather the spider that surprises you be poisonous or not, matters little to one with a sturdy foundation.

Gardener at Dust

The setting sun paints everything.
The ugly becomes beautiful.
The beautiful becomes golden.
The brutality of man is stolen.
The sun glows red, you feel nature in your soul.
All that is life is in the soil you mold.
You harbor no ill will, only light.
So precious is this magical twilight.
The sky turns purple as the sun peeks before bed.
Your heart sings because it is glad.
The birds make their final flight.
Their grace stills your mind as you ponder the sight.
Twilight merges into dusk.
And you are in tune with the sounds that come forth.
You marvel that with so much to treasure.
Why In hate do we find so much pleasure?

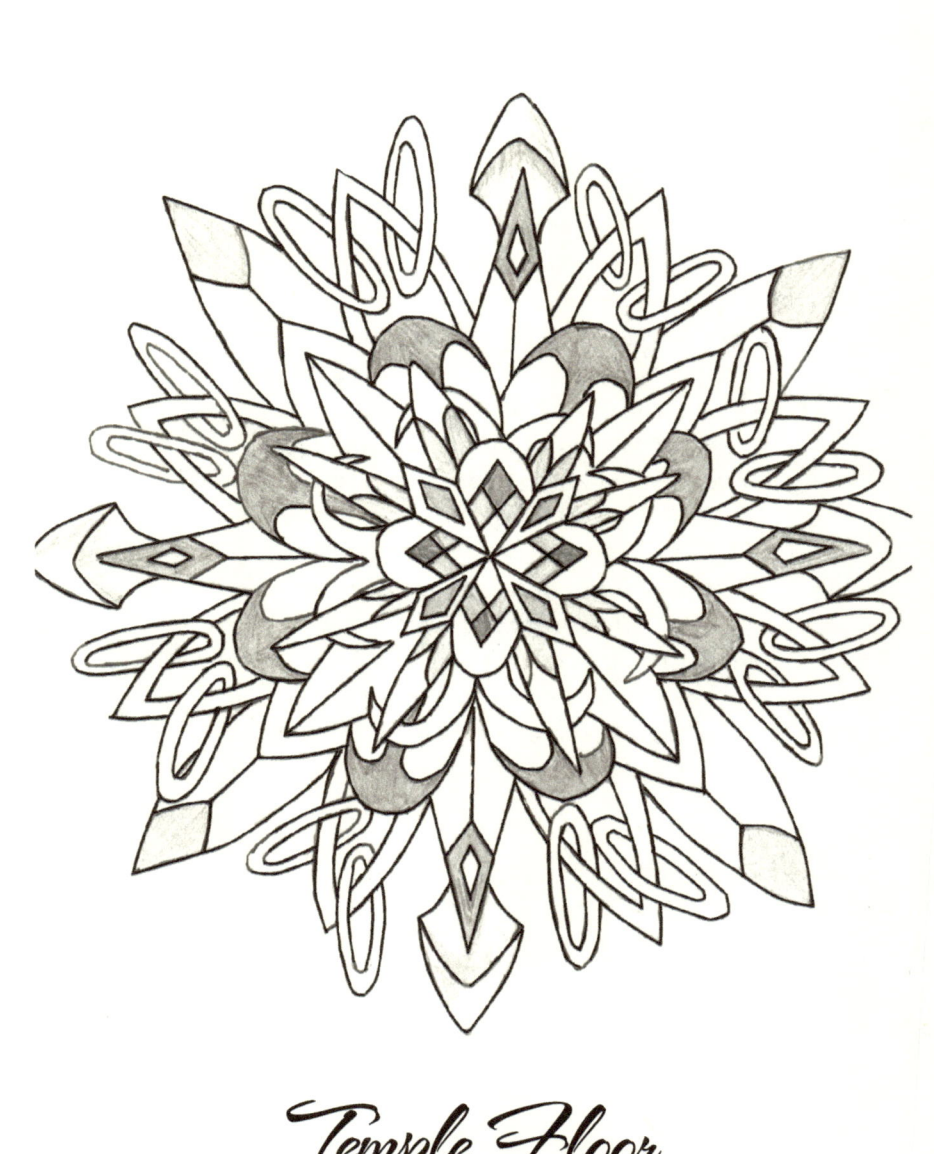

Temple Floor

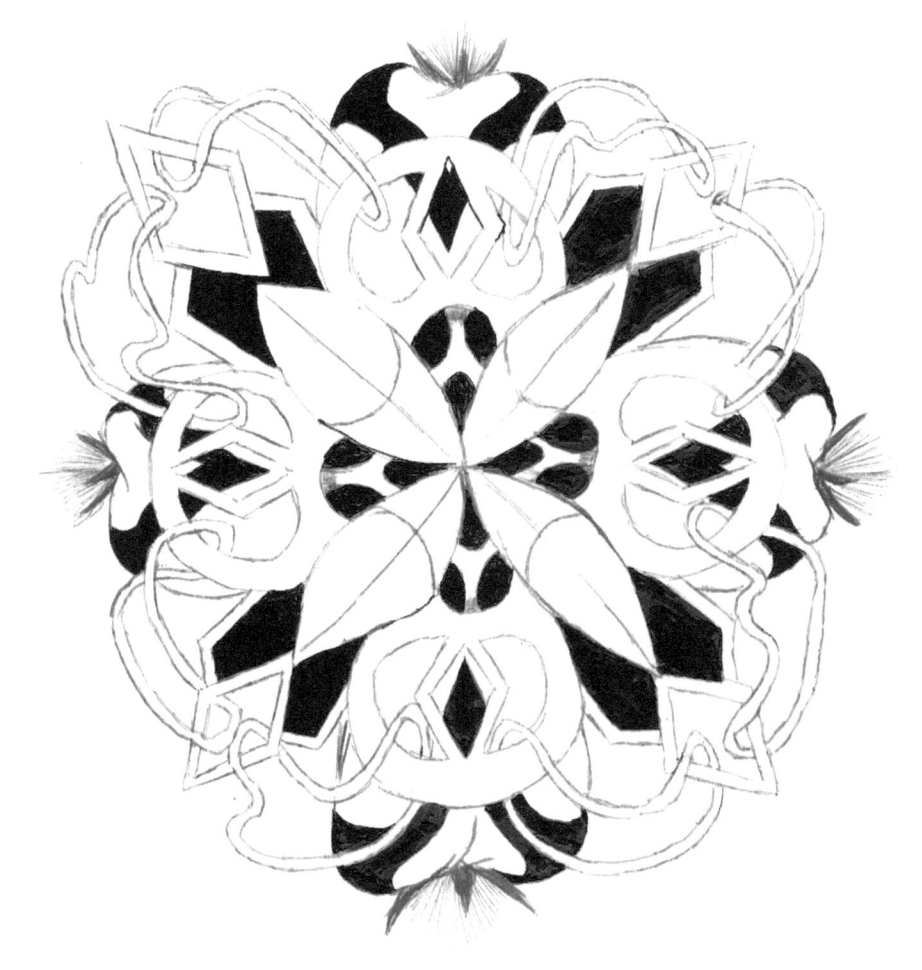

Military Apple

This medal is awarded to people good at sherking their duties, gold bricking and just general laziness. They amuse and make you laugh. But when it is time to go home you notice they haven't done anything. But you don't mind because they are fun people and their jesting makes the job go faster. So while you work hard and earn your pay, they grin and clown to retirement without ever working a single day.

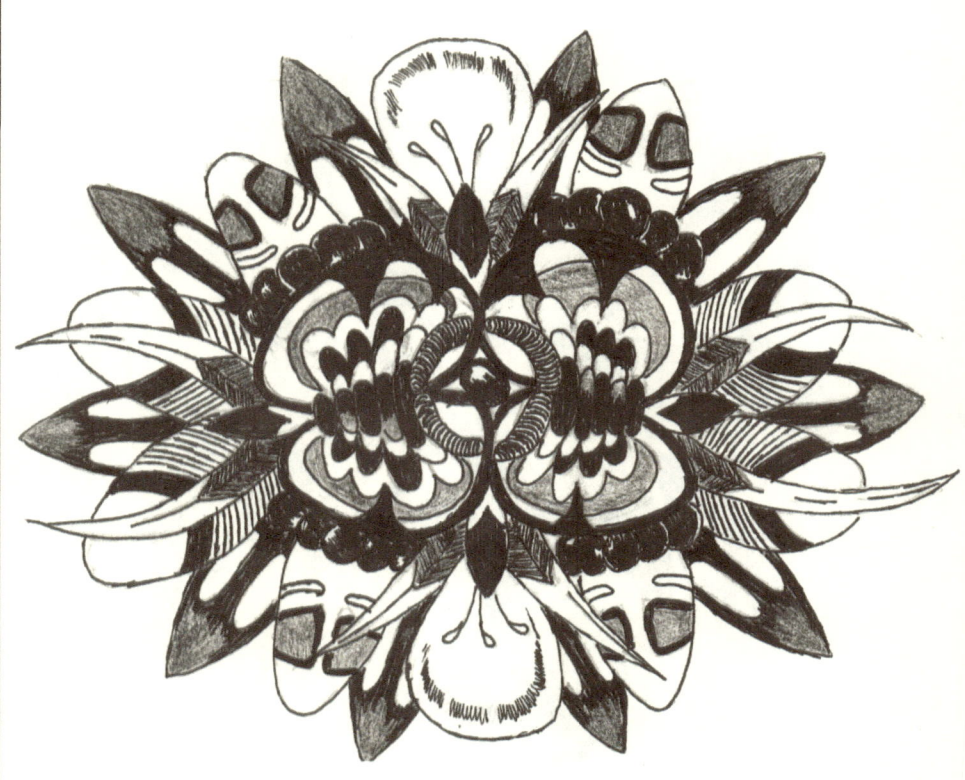

African Butterfly

I am african american. Therefore I of african descent. Ask me what country in africa I am from, I will tell you I. do not know. Ask me what african tribe I am from, I will tell you I do not know. Ask me if I feel african, I will tell you I do not know.

Stationed Away

I wish I was there, that goes without saying.
To be stationed near you, is for what I am praying.
Together forever, we will be staying.
Now these aren't just words you hear me saying.
In my heart and mind they do live.
And my life for you I will give.
And I hope that it is clear, you will never hear me say I am out of here.
Marriages come and marriages go.
But count on our marriage to thrive and grow.

Giving In

From behind me, her soft quiet voice settled upon me like warm ocean spray.
I would like to know your thoughts, she said.
Tantalized I turned quickly, anticipating pleasure for my weary eyes and at the same time hoping I wasn't wrong again.
Her beauty hit me hard like sunshine piercing my soul.
She smiles at my helplessness.
But I don't care that she knows that I am instantly and totally hers.
Rather she feels the same way is not important.
There is no way I cannot love her. My emotions are beyond my control.
I've seen you here before, alone, on the beach staring out over the water.
I can feel the incompleteness of your existence.
It is similar to mines, she said.
Her words permeate me like the influence of fine wine.
I drink them in thirstily and they soothe me for their essence sing in harmony with my desires.
Her hand reaches out and tenderly caresses my cheek.
Her delegate fingers float over invisible lines that mark the tracks of my tears.
Does she know? How could she?
My sorrow fades into echoes of yesterday.
I fall willingly into eyes that can only belong to an angle.
Somewhere inside a part of me screams don't be silly, don't be venerable.
But I ignore it as so much irrelevant noise.
Who notices the sound of a door closing when a full orchestra is beautifully assaulting your senses?
I grasp the hand upon my cheek and press is lightly to my lips.
I have no secret because I belong to her. Do with me what you wish, I concede.
I shall she concurs and my heart sings.

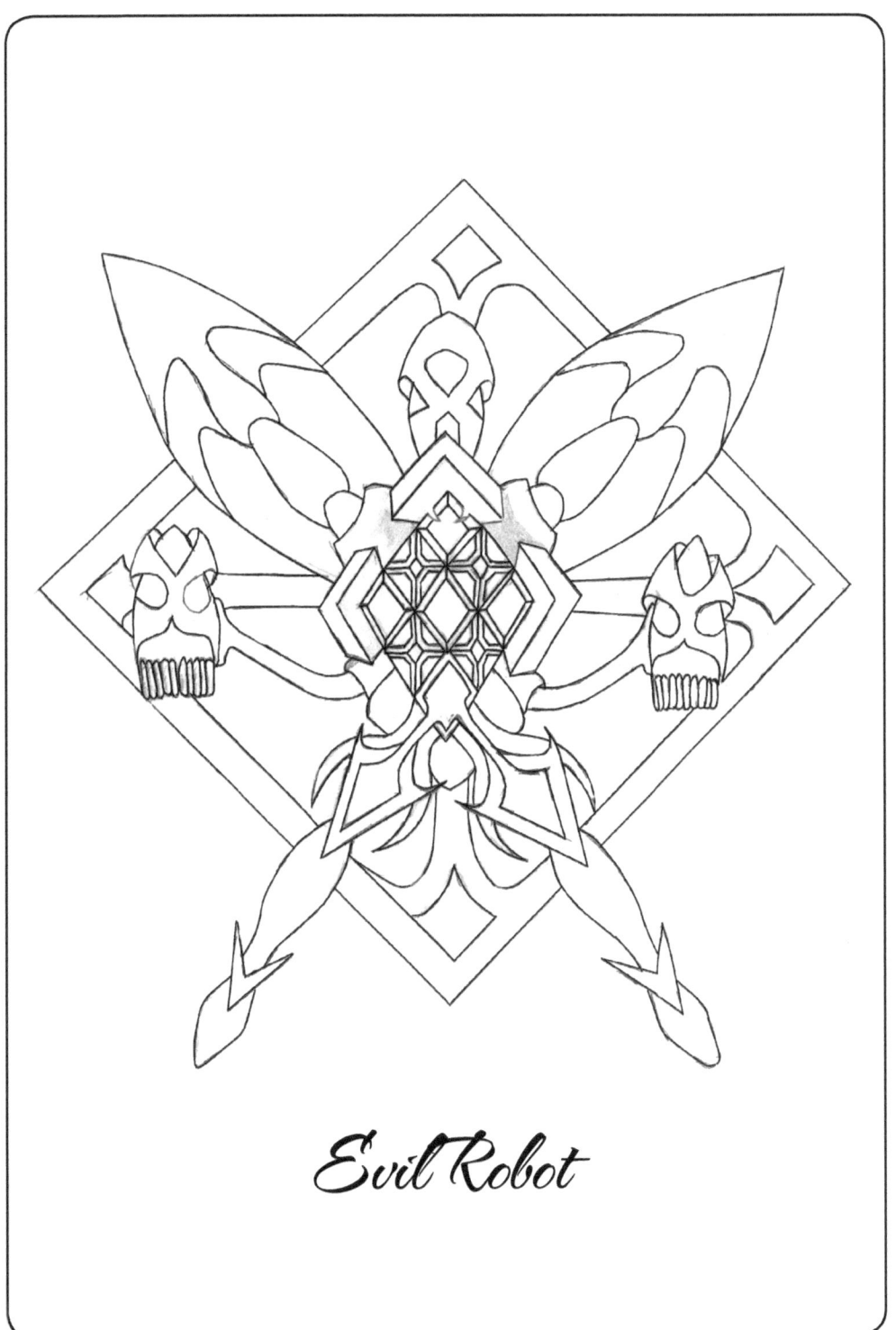

Evil Robot

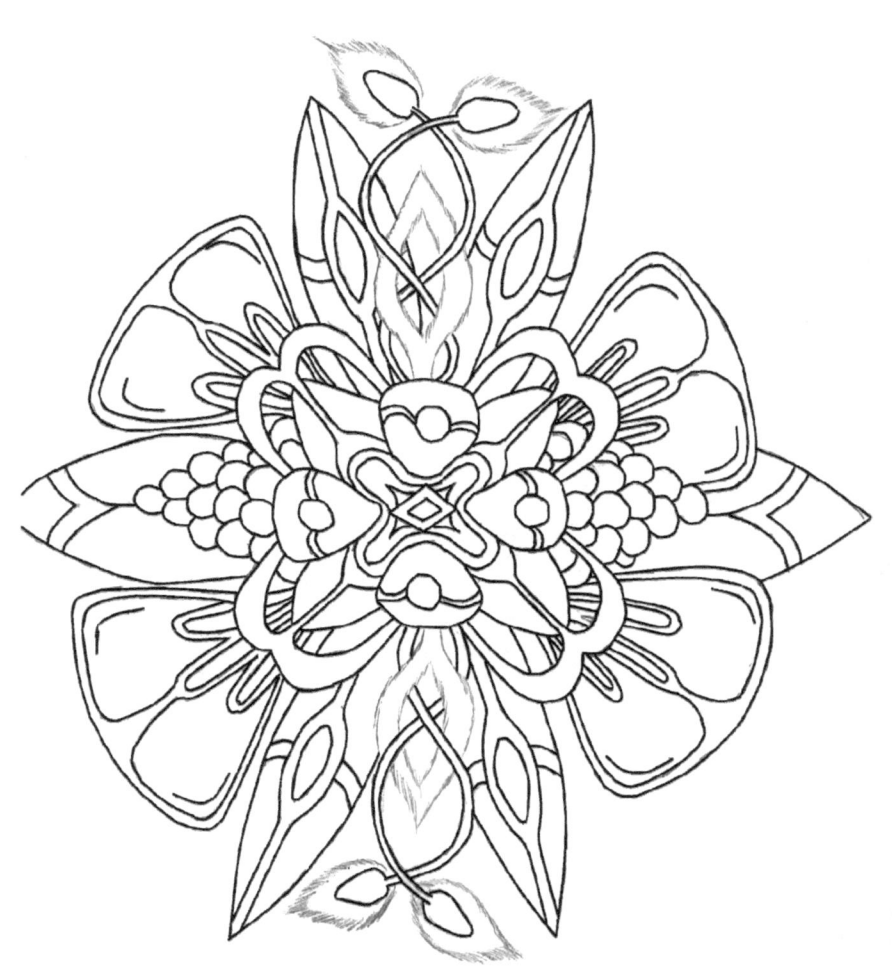

Easter

Begin again, begin a new. Is this what Easter means to you. Sweep away the mess. Get the weight off your chest. Do you really think you are doing your best?

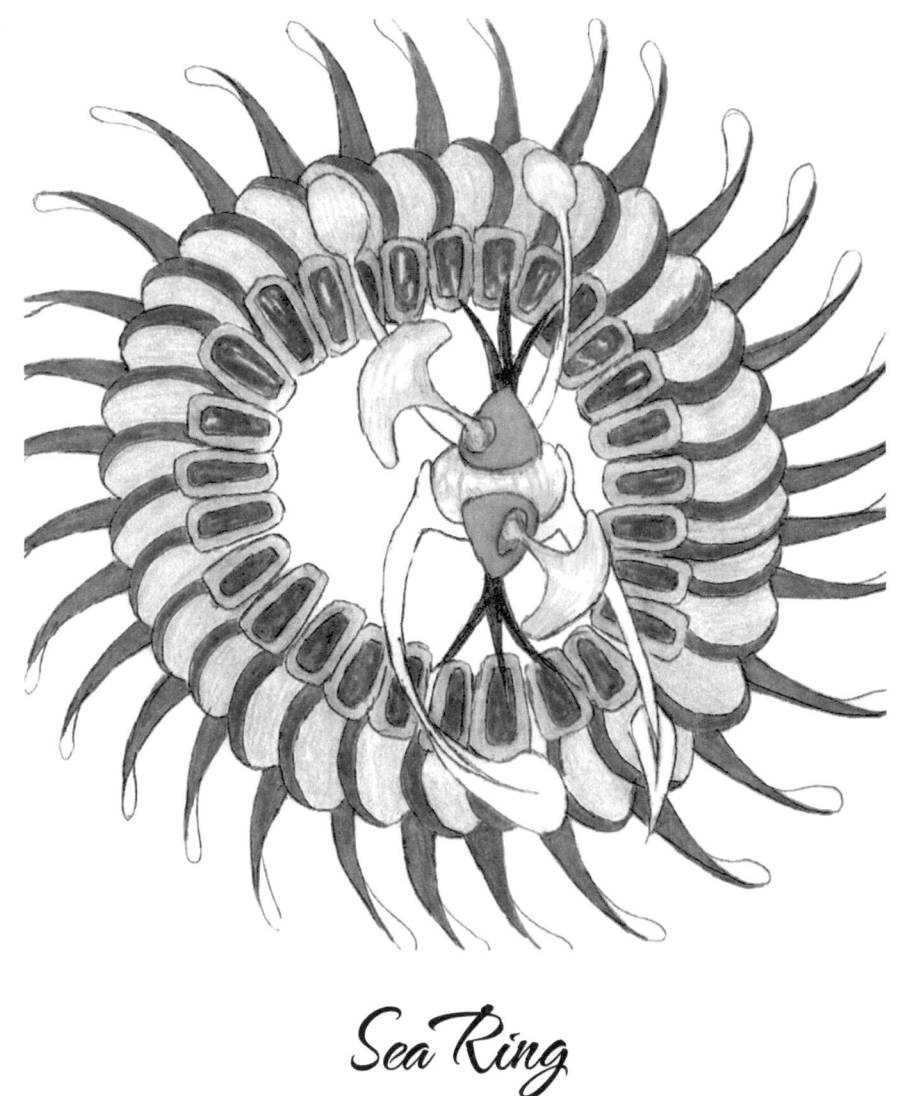

Sea Ring

The sea ring lives in eternal darkness at the bottom of the ocean. It swims with its internal organs exposed. It has no fear. Ocean dwellers acclimated to the sea ring's domain, don't know what to make of it. They eye it suspiciously. Surely it must have a trick up its sleeve. Nothing can be so oblivious that it goes around boldly with its vital organs on display. It must have some unseen fantastic defense, they reason. So they never test it. They always steer clear, never knowing its only defense is their confusion.

Invisible Enemy

Sitting back, looking around, you see, there is a new player in town.
Like Miami Vice, scoping out the scene, breaking new ice.
This is old hat. I don't let the situation play me.
I am a larceny gypsy, tried and true.
I know the game and have mastered the rules.
An invisible enemy is the way I am known.
No one knows me. There is no one I owe.
My face will never be seen.
I know my place. I am behind the scene.
I am faster than lighting but I don't strike twice.
I keep you guessing and my timing tight.
To disguise my move, I blind you with hype
I only attack when the time is ripe.
Before you know, the game is through, and you beaten but by who?
You remember how you laughed when you were told,
The player was jacking people up, knocking people down.
It is too late to cry because you got a raw deal.
You were warned but you did not believe the threat was real
I can't be beat because my weapon is my mind.
My tools are time and surprise.
You won't see me coming.
You won't know I am there.
I am impossible to grasp, I am like air.

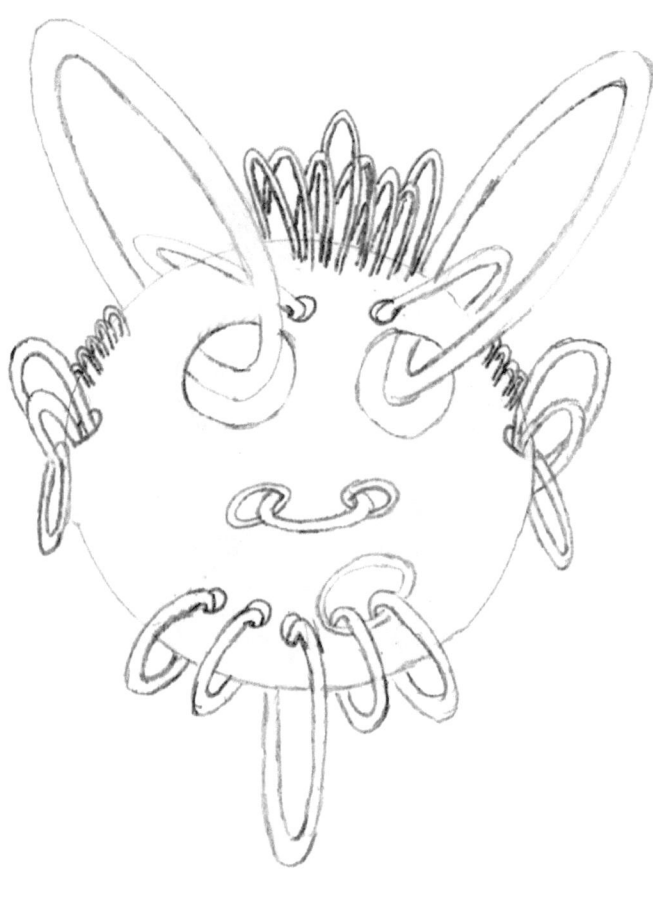

More Rings Please

To avoid extremes, everything should be in moderation.

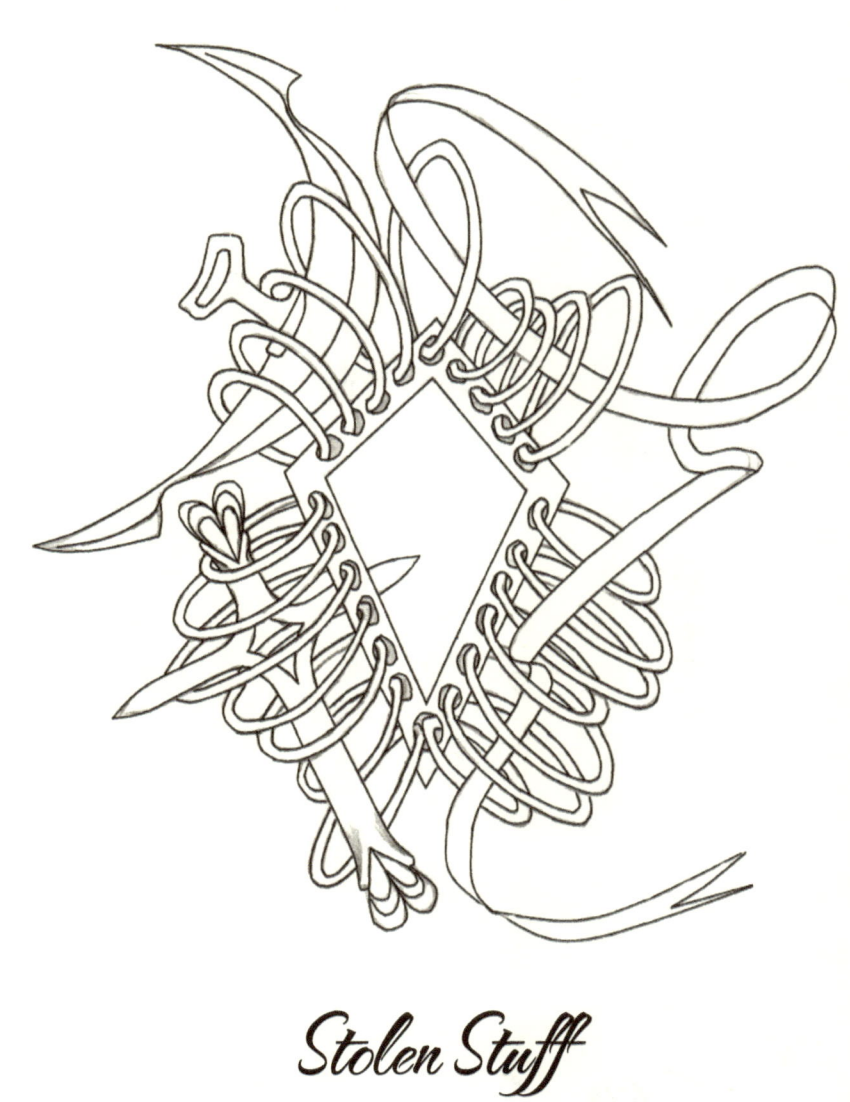

Stolen Stuff

Things that we value, time that we want, thoughts that are precious, are all taken by the stress of life and hidden from us until they become obscure mist of memories. Only in times when the weight of living becomes too much do we search our minds for those stolen items because they are meaningful, spirit substaining and rejuvenating.

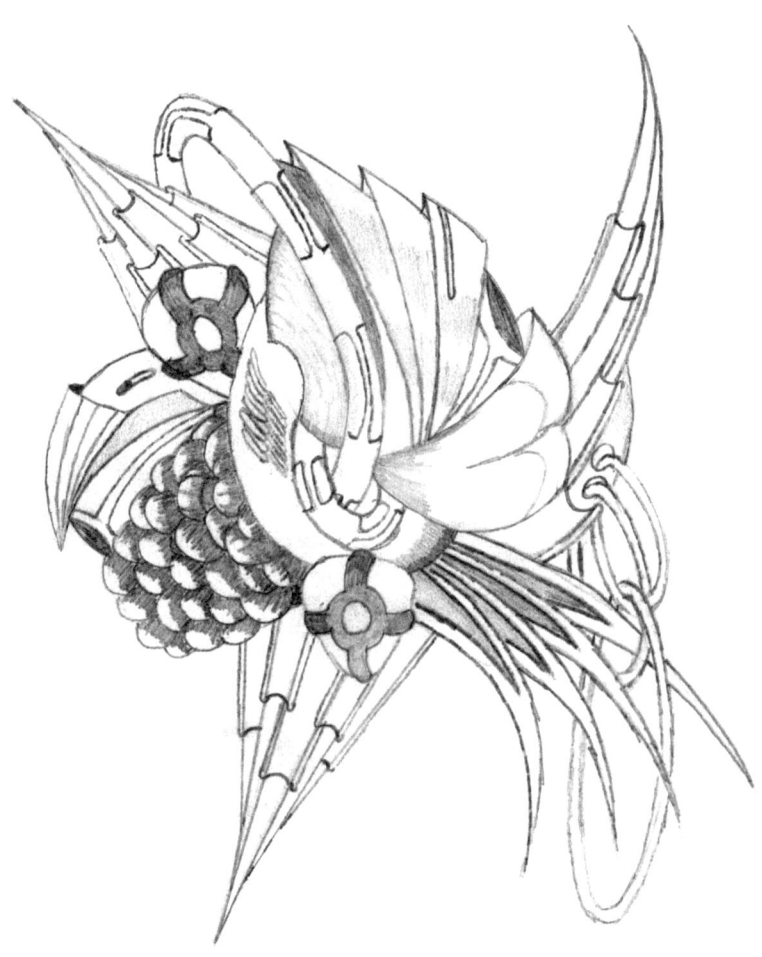

Star Searcher

Always seeking but never finding. Regardless, always optimistic, always persistent. Not even sure of what it is looking for. But is sure the journey is worthwhile because it is sure it doesn't want to be where it has been.

Invisible

Who saw me coming?
I think no one.
And when I did get noticed, they saw my body but they didn't see me.
They heard my voice but they didn't hear my words.
I felt invisible, I was invisible, I did not exist.
It is hard to find yourself when you can't see yourself.
Through other people's eyes I had to stop looking.
I can't depend on their vision to lead me the right way.
Too often they step on me to feel good about themselves.
All you invisible people out there, stop seeing yourself through others.
Look in the mirror.
It is not scary at all.

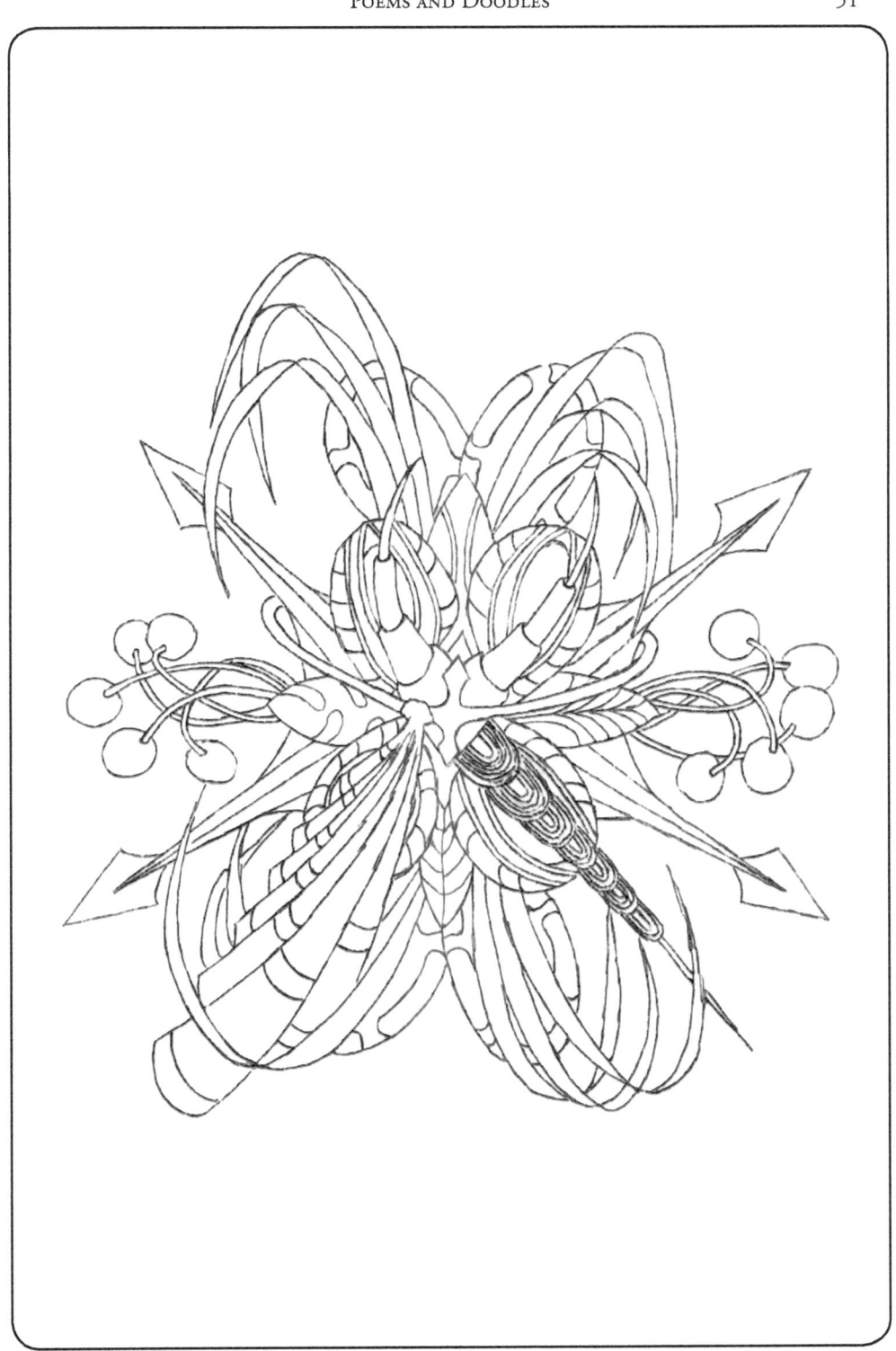

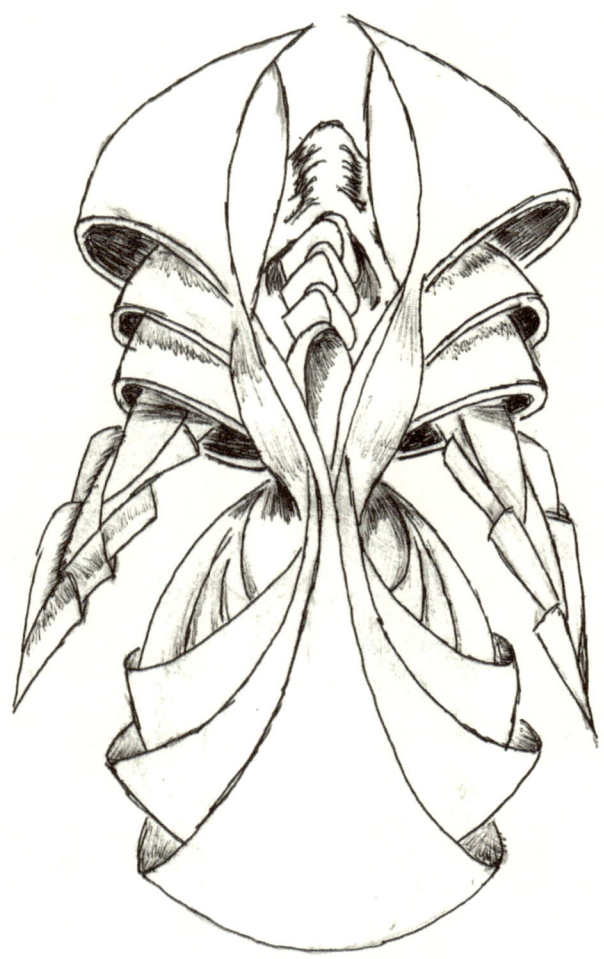

Menace

If you are a bad person your heart is his home. The dark aura you create when you do wrong, feeds him and makes him strong. So think twice before robbing and thieving. Because once he is in he ain't leaving. And when your essence is sucked dry. You will feel you want to die. Right will become wrong and wrong will become right. And only ugly will fill your sight.

It is just a thing

It sits there, a big thing in the water.
The crew calls it by name, implying that it is alive.
Implying that it can think, feel, get angry, become glad.
They call it he or she, the pig, Mary P, the hog, the dog.
All it is to me is a bit piece of metal sitting in the water.
It has various protrusions like small boats, a boom, a winch.
But no arms head or legs.
It only moves when we start the engines.
It only goes where we steer.
It doesn't take care of itself.
We do up keep and repair.
The crew speaks of it as though it has influence over our lives.
This relationship I don't understand,
Maybe that is why she makes me sea sick and hates my love of land.

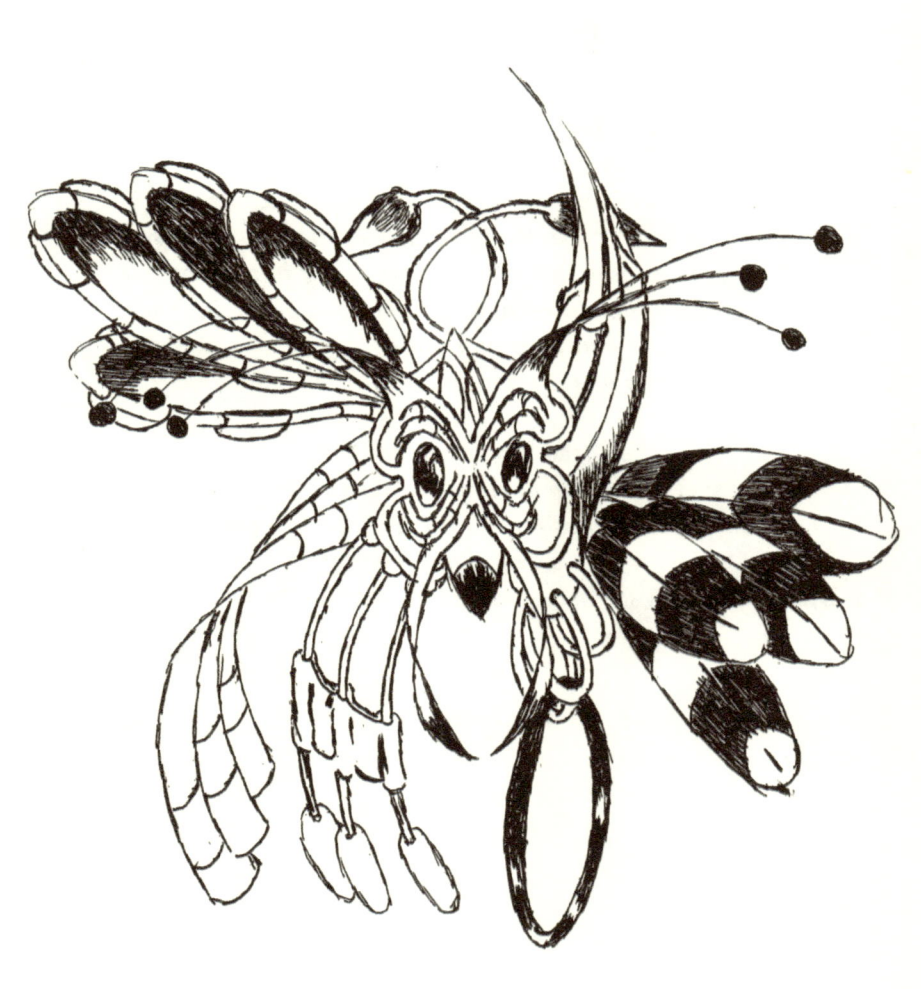

Cattle Skull

Work Morning Blues

Up in the morning, hoping for a sunrise,
out the window, only dreary gray clouds.
I sit on the bedside.
I want to close my eyes.
It is a struggle not snuggle my pillow once again.
A pot of coffee later, I still got the blues.
I shuffle to the bathroom, listening to the new.
When the water is warm,
I step under and drift off into a world where,
there is no office or boss to wear me down,
there is no competition to get a higher position.
There is no fight to all ways be right.
I come out of my world.
And Friday seems light years away.
I step outside and start my day.

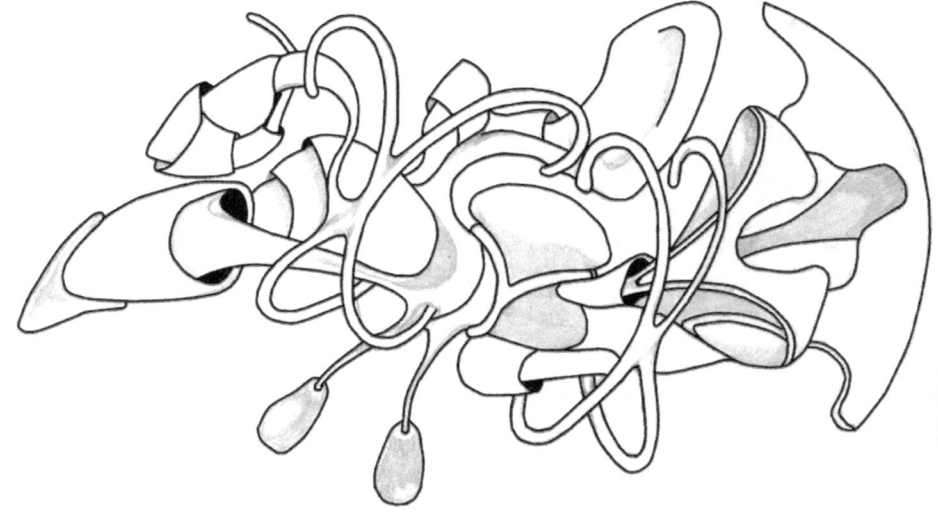

Energy Drawer

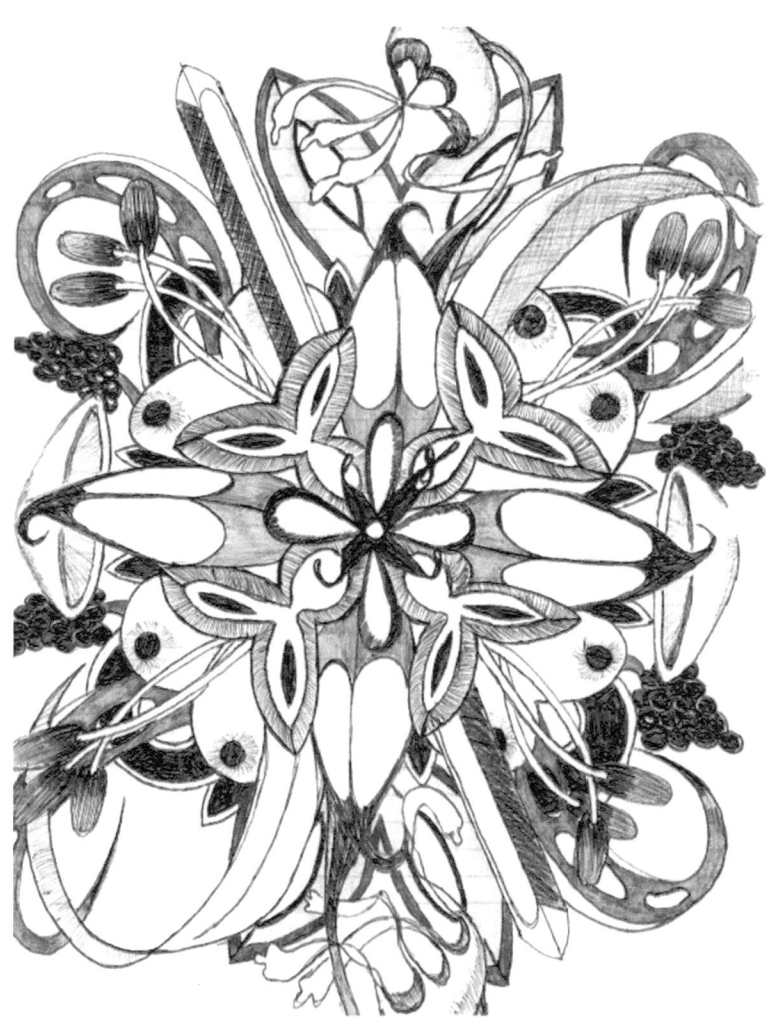

Rasberry Flower

The sword and the flower. Or as Asians say, the Yin and the Yang. We in the west thing power and peace. They all are two sides of the same coin. One cannot exist without the other. Indeed, one might say they are brothers.

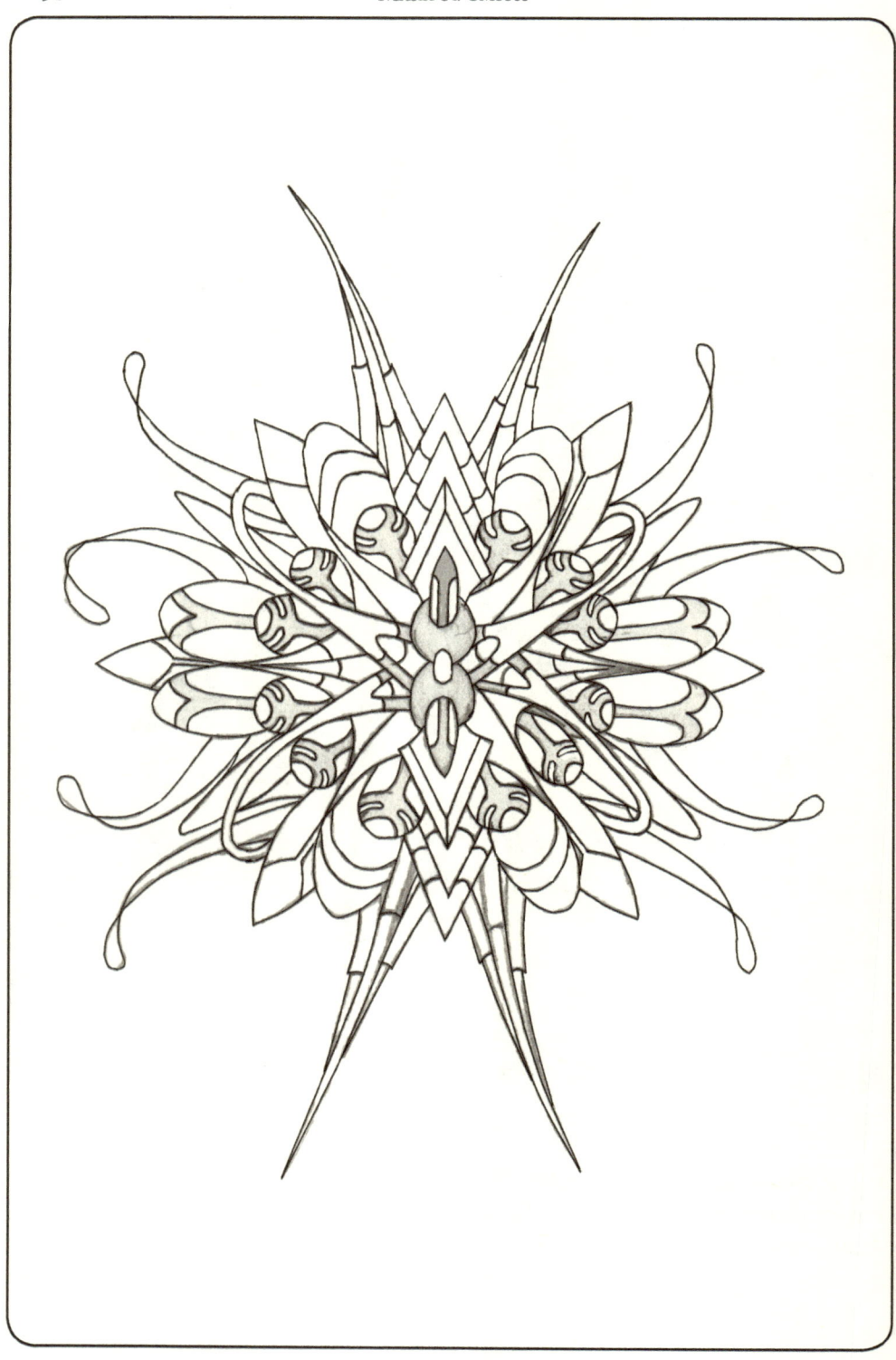

Just Choose Dummy

Which path should I take?
Such a heavy choice,
What if I choose wrong?
And make a mistake.
At times like this I remember the words,
Of the great and wise Fred Sanford,
Just choose dummy.

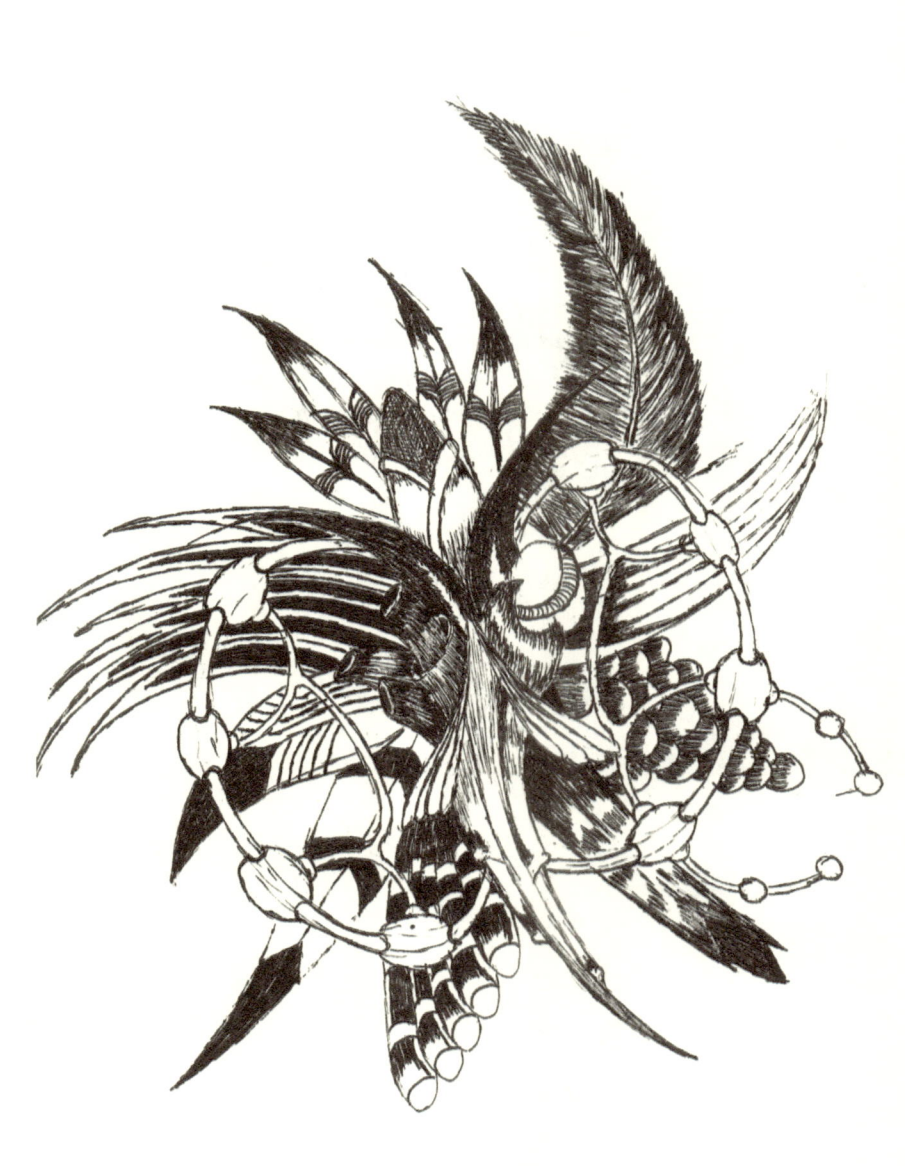

Bird's Nest

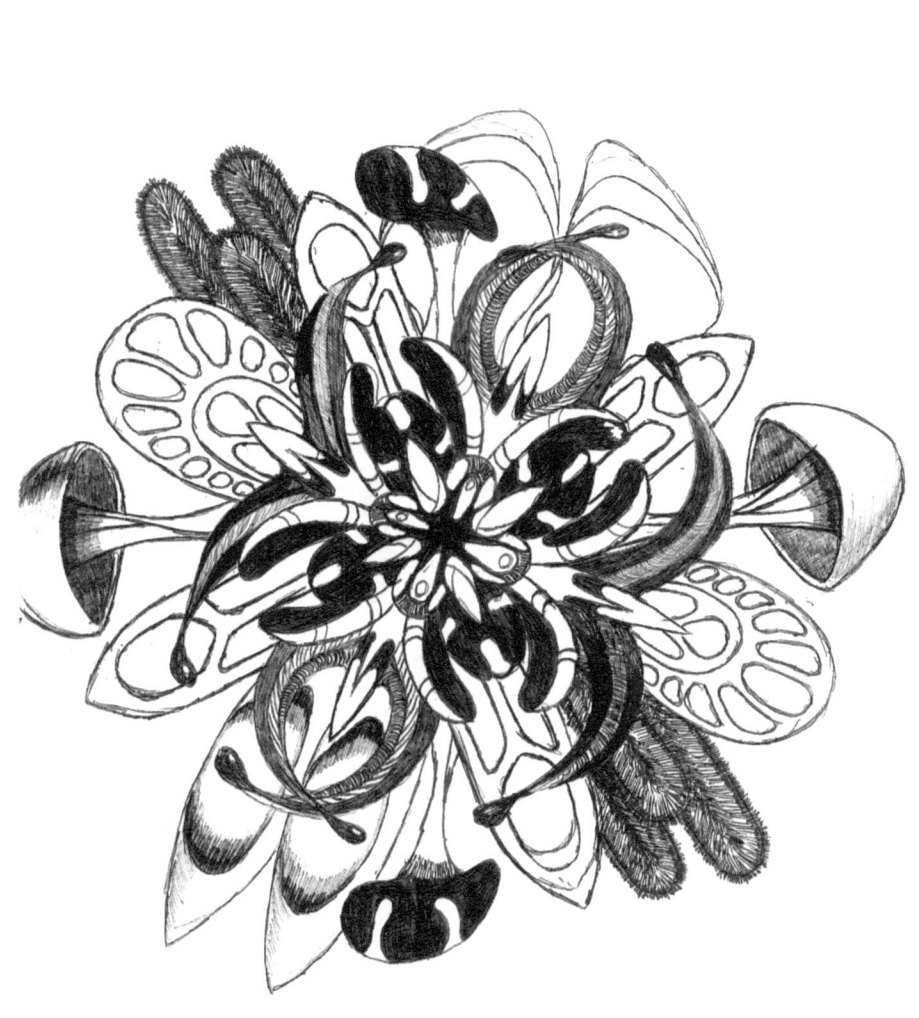

Mushroom

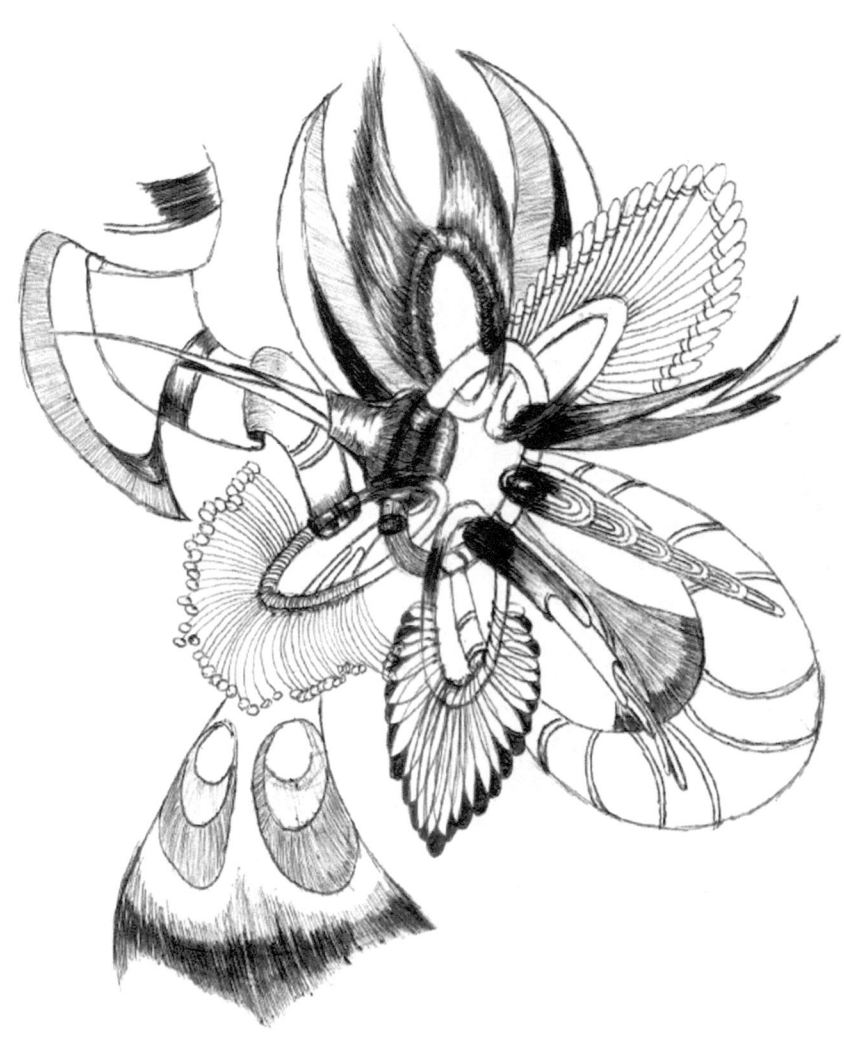

Shaman's Key Ring

Just Leave

I don't care about what you want.
I don't care about what you need.
Baby, just leave.

You say you want it to work out.
You would like to grow old with me.
But how can that be,
when you can't stand the sight of me.
Just leave.

Respect, you have none.
So baby just walk,
God speed.
Can't you see,
the solution,
is to just leave.

When I hold you tight,
it doesn't feel right.
When I come into the room,
you start a fight.
I don't know if you are cheating,
But won't tell me where you go.
It seems you are always walking out the door.
Next time, keep walking, just go.

I no longer care about what you want.
I don't care about what you need.
Just leave.

Despite what you say, you don't want to be here.
I am not the one you want.
I am not the one you need.
Do yourself a favor and just leave.

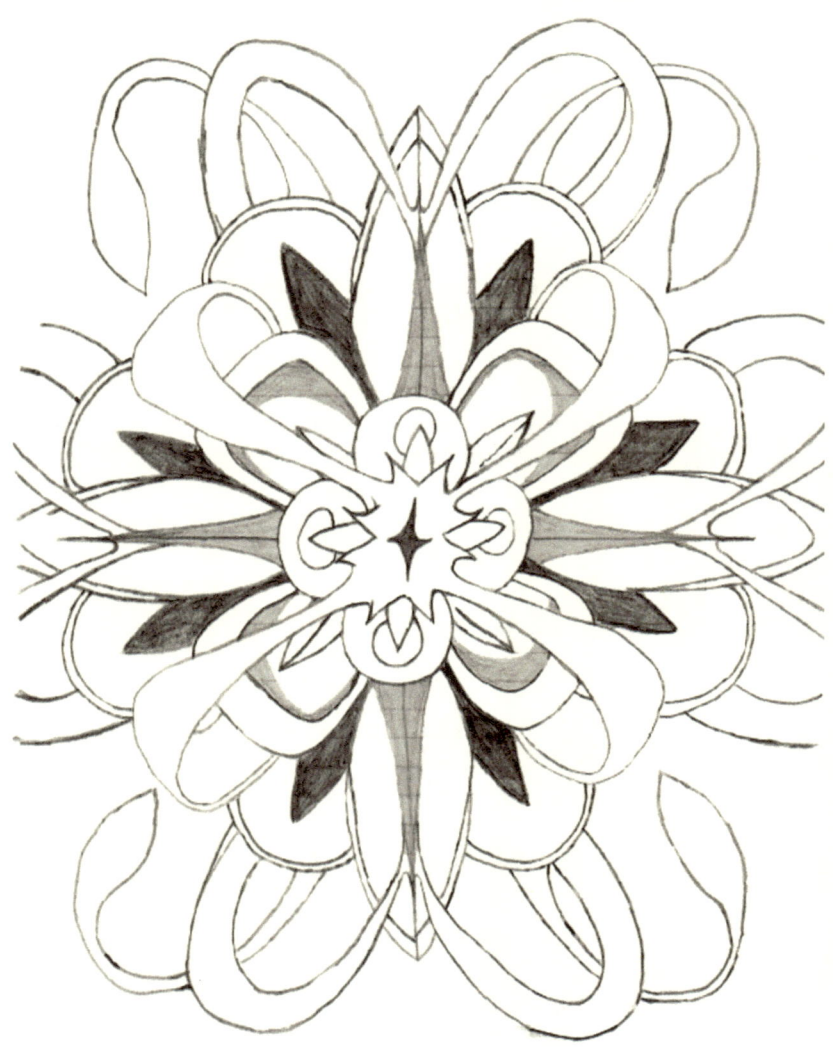

Bow

Some days you know from the beginning are going to be special. You wake up feeling full of life. The sky is brilliantly blue. Everything you do turns out right. These days are presents special delivered wrapped up with a bow.

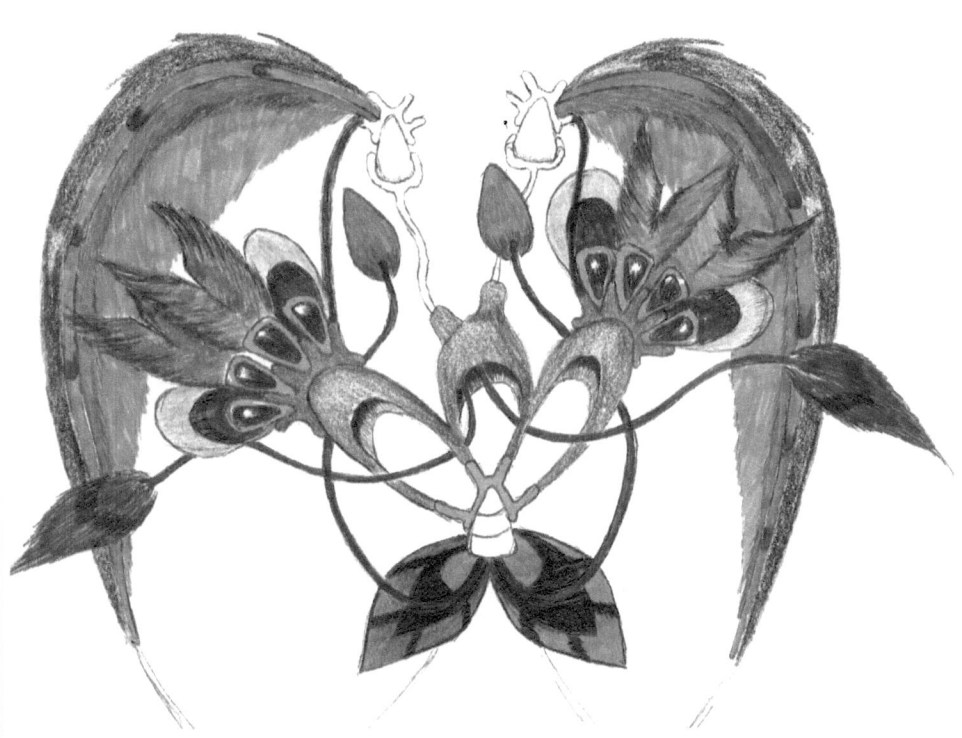

A Game

Patroling the coast of Haiti, there is no danger, Haiti has no navy. The danger is ashore. US Coast Guard Port Security Units are there, and they brought their A game. Me? I just languish on patrol, what a bore.

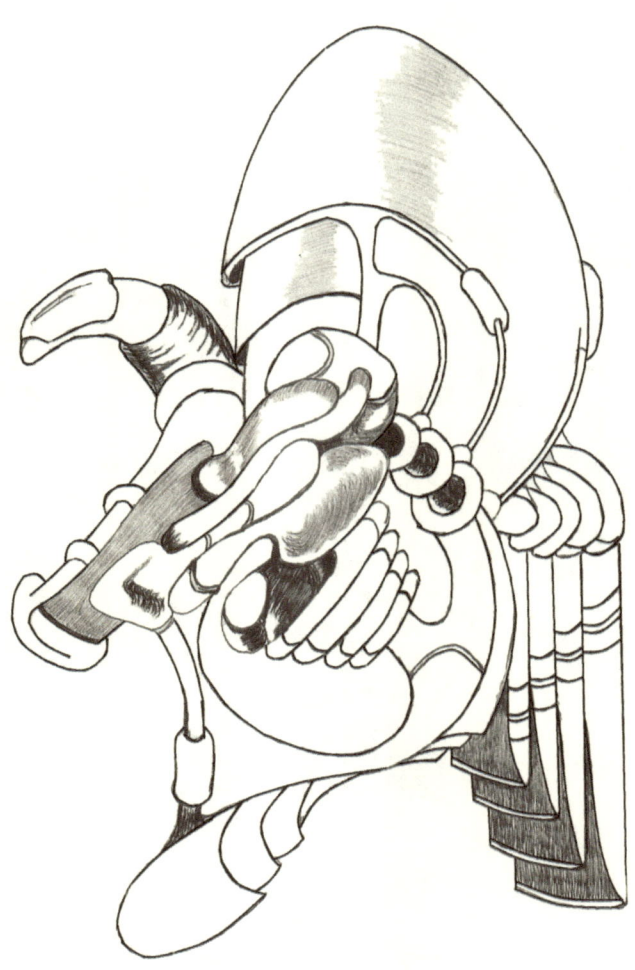

Alien Device

Analyze, survey, surveillance, what is necessary to determine if it should save or destroy. It has been sent to journey the universe, unattended, unmonitored. It acts on its own volition, guided by preset rules. What makes it so frightening is once a determination has been made, no amount of negotiation will sway it.

Pathetic Existence

It is summertime and the dope heads are out.
It makes you mad to see people living so bad.
On the streets, in the parks, everywhere you turn,
they are hunting for the dope man.
Your attempts to help them have been futile.
You wish there was something you could do, to shield their
pathetic existence from view.
A cold beer would take your mind off the gloom they inspire.
So you cruise down to the bar, intending to throw back just a few.
But since you just broke up with your girl you are feeling blue.
You see some friends, they drink with you.
You talk about your jobs which none of you like.
You switch to hard liquor to ease the bite of life.
You run out of hard money and go to credit.
But the bartenders don't trust you, so you must beg him to let you.
Several hours later you stumble from the closed bar.
But you have enough sense to leave your car.
You're not ready to go home and face the memories of your girl.
So you head for a liquor store on Blake and Pearl.
On shaky legs you begin to walk and to yourself you begin to talk.
You argue with the woman you no longer have.
And long for more liquor into which to dive.
It is your intension to urgently drown the pathetic existence
to which you belong.

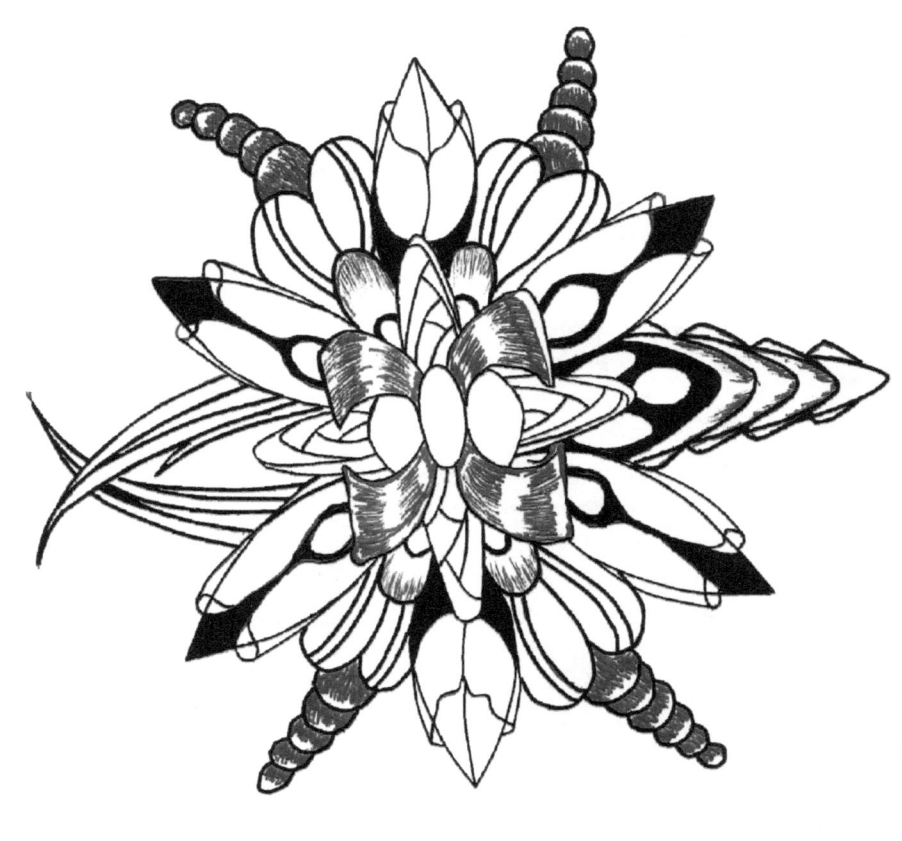

Award Ribbon

Pretty Soft Thing

He thought he was smiling, but it was only a sneer, a sneer from ear to ear.
He thought he was suave, but he was only a snob,
a snob who held nothing below him dear.
He thought he dressed well but he only paid well,
for clothes that looked good in the dark.
He called himself fair, but he really only cared about the size of his bank account.
At last for all he pictured himself to be, the picture was not complete.
He had to have and vowed one day to find a pretty, soft thing.
He brought women by the truck load, four and five a night.
But their numbers could not quiet his ferocious appetite.
Once used, they lay about, like empty shells, tired and spent.
He would sit staring, thinking this is what hell sent.
His money did not draw honey but rather bitter fruit.
But still he reasoned money was needed to continue his pursuit.
At last he could not see himself, though there were many mirrors around.
He looked in them but only saw fairy tales abound.
He dealt harshly with those who crossed him, because his heart was full of pain
Pain he was sure would ease with a pretty soft thing.
He spied a woman one night. So pure and young she did appear. He could not
believe the line of work she was in.
He paid her price and took her home, hoping this would be it.
He treated her so kindly she thought surely something was amiss.
After dinner and wine and conversation by the fire,
the woman asked him point blank.
Are you a stud or queer, which is it dear and spanking is surely out.
Those words from her mouth so pretty and small didn't seem appropriate at all.
But still he hoped and tried to make the most of this woman of call.
Pray tell me please, why can't I partake of the seed,
which blooms one as lovely as you?
She thought for a minute and in her eyes there was pity
and gently she took his hand.
To mate with a dove you must be a dove. Do you understand?

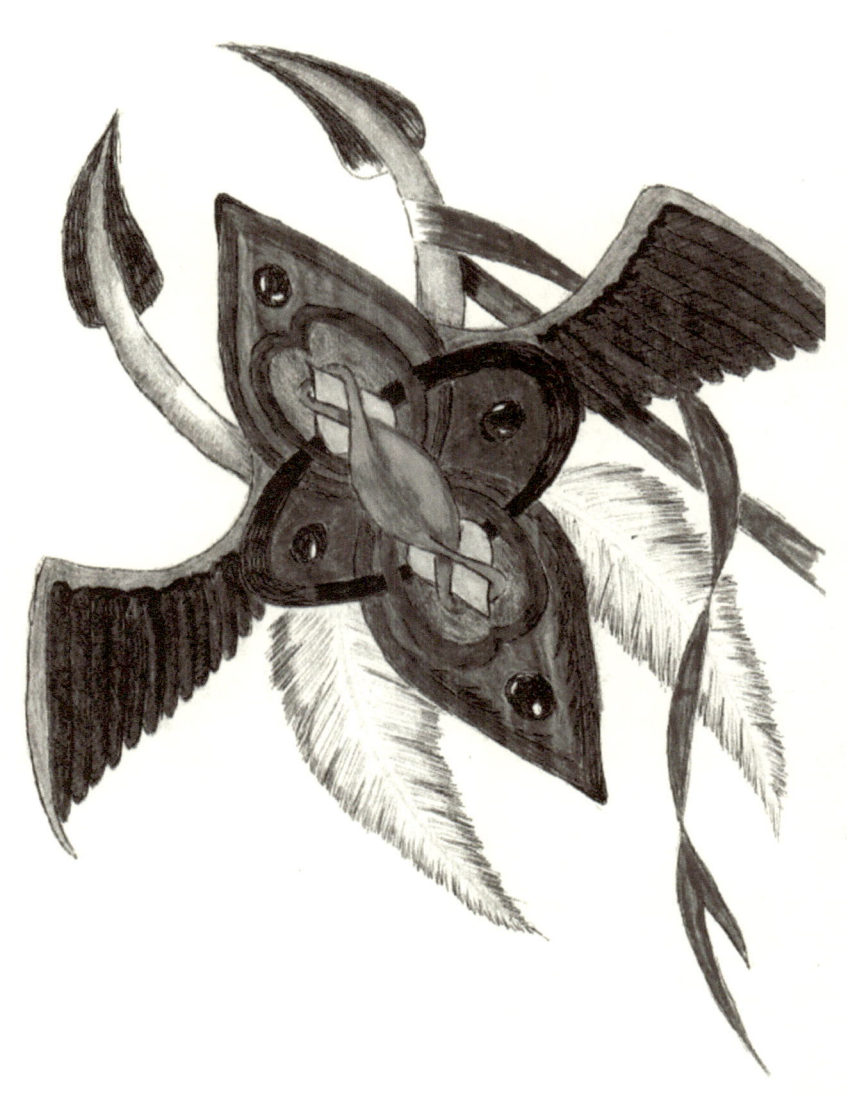

Bloodlust Beetle

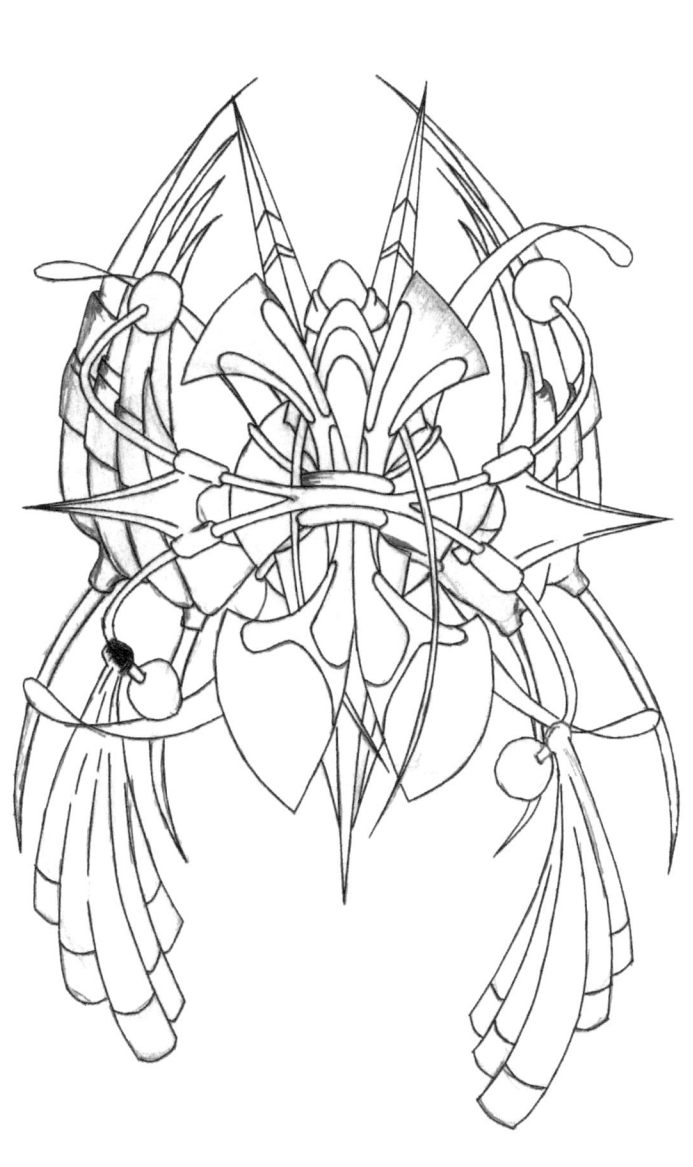

Cherry Bomb

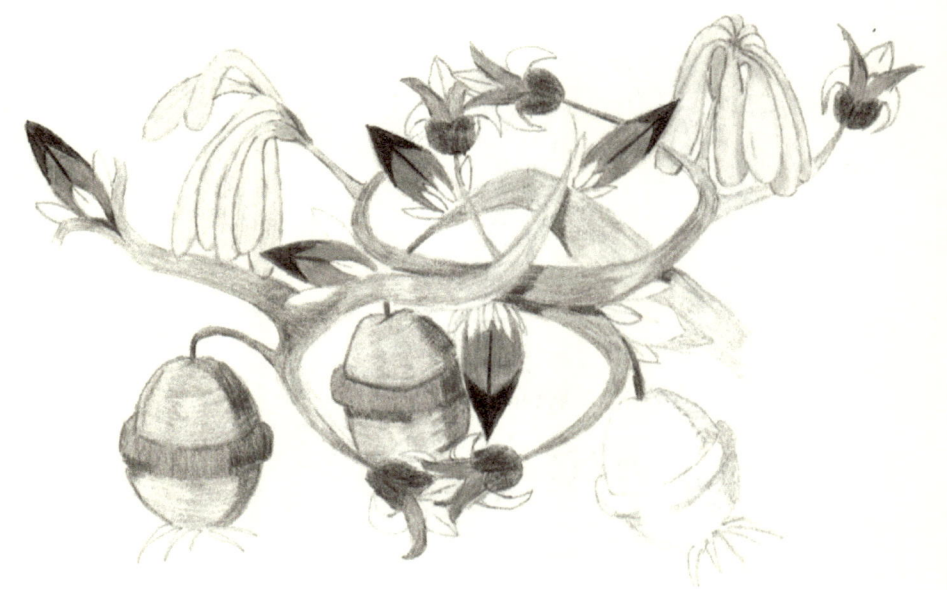

Drean Friut

So I saw this dog with golden fur.
He came up to me happily wagging his tail.
It was a golden day, out of a golden week.
And none of this goldeness did I seek.

Sensitive Man

Do you like sex?
Surprised by the question, modesty caused her eyes to blink.
Nervously she checked to see,
if embarrassment was warranted.
But no curious stares found her.
Upon her face Irritation found a home.
What manner of fool had she taken into her confidence she wondered?
Her whisper was a heated hiss as she said,
Couldn't you find a better way to ask?
I thought you were nice,
I thought you were smart.
Now I see you are not.
Flustered by her stern aberrance, up from the table he sprung.
Angry words in his mind could not find his lips.
So he stammered incoherently before one of those angry words spilled out.
Rotten whore he screamed.
Heads turned towards the disturbance.
I am a sensitive man, how dare you be so harsh.
Inappropriate behavior people gasped.
Were they speaking of his behavior or hers, the woman did not know.
Dutifully she felt shame for them both.
Unaware of anything except his indignation,
More horrid words used to describe her, he spit into the air.
Until, finally without fanfare the woman stood.
And in her hand a gun appeared.
The man fell silent.
His legs walked him back away from the threat.
Her face gave no indication that she fired twice.
Upon the man who now lay upon the ground she did not look.
There was nothing there she wanted to see.

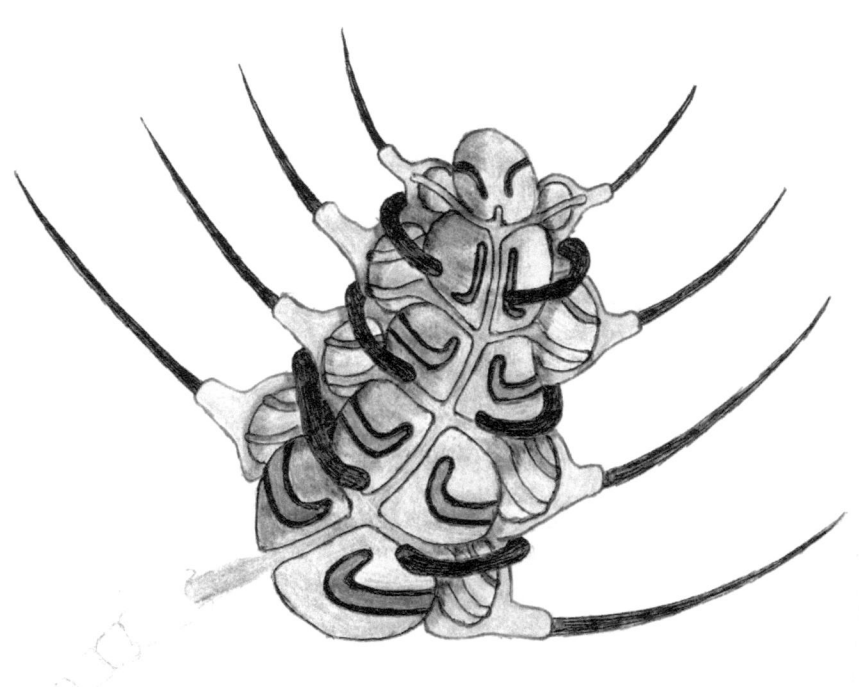

Face Lice

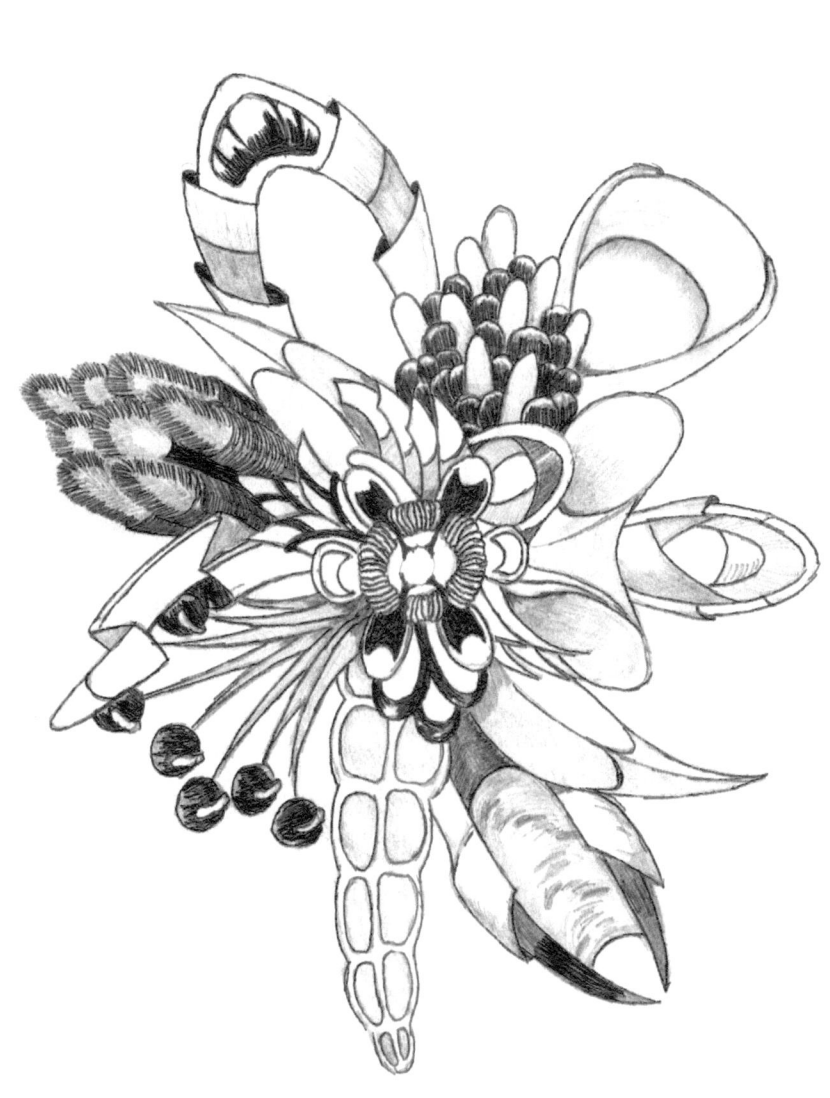

Grim Ornament

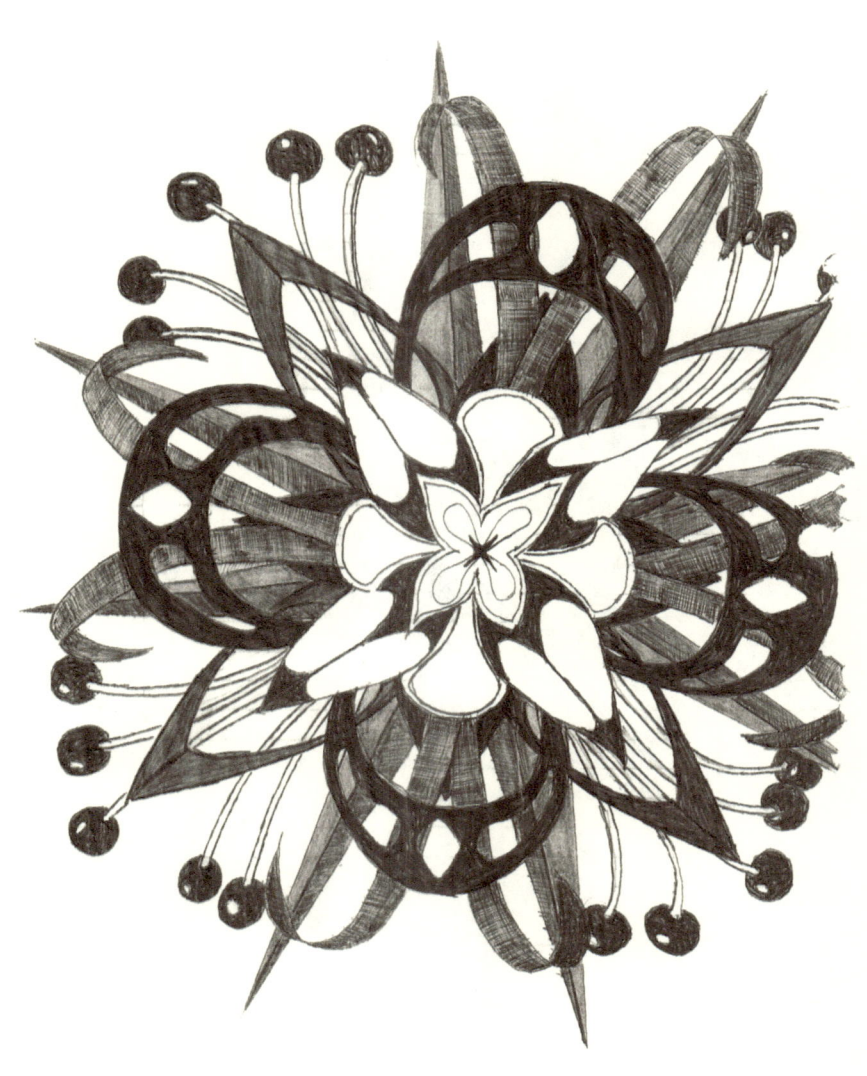

Lattice

Something Somebody

People pass to and fro, so many feet,
not seeing the smelly clump sitting upon the street.
He doesn't know where they are going. Nor from whence they come.
He is just amazed at their automation.
They pass him by and if one chance to glance in his eyes they see,
Something someone told him long before he had fleas.
But the glance is just a glance, it is not long enough to read,
so he pays it little attention, takes no heed.
But each time it happens, something stirs inside.
This something somebody told him keeps bothering him why?
I am happy with myself, he begs for a dime.
I don't want to be a part of that, to buy a bottle of wine.
There is nothing I want, nothing I desire.
The wine, he hopes, will take him higher.
In his drunken stupor he can still see the street.
He is having nightmares about those damn feet.
He sits up in a haze.
A woman gives him one of those glances.
And on her face he feels like dancing.
But the moment flees with the dizziness of the wine.
And he starts to wonder what was that something somebody told him, while
still had his whole mind.
He thought and he thought, what a strain on the brain.
He turned the bottle up again and the last of the wine he drained.
He tried hard to pull it out, he really wanted to see what it was about.
Then after one last pull with all his might, that something somebody told him
came into the light.
His eyes clouded over, his hands curled into fist.
He wished he had left it buried in the mist.
He turned up his bottle, but nothing was inside.
And he wondered when they told him he could never fly.

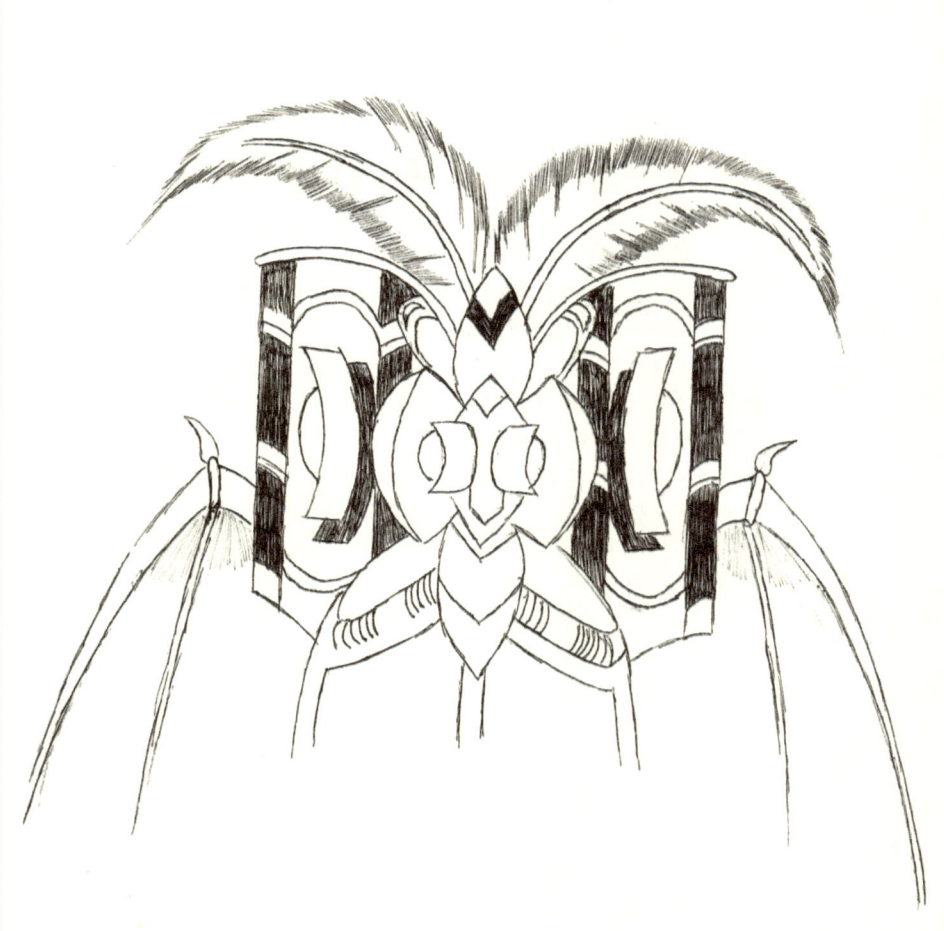

Mask

Wouldn't it be great to wear an all powerful mask?
With the mask on you could do anything, from creating world peace being good at math.
But would you put the mask on if you could never take it off?

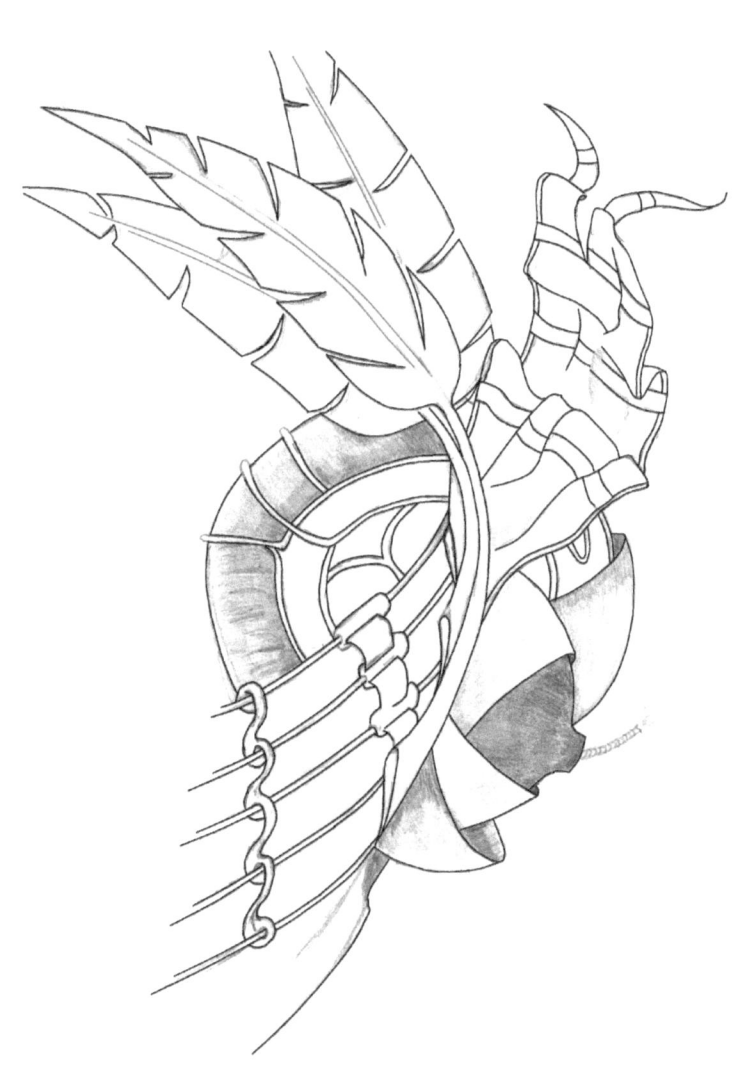

Pirate's Crest

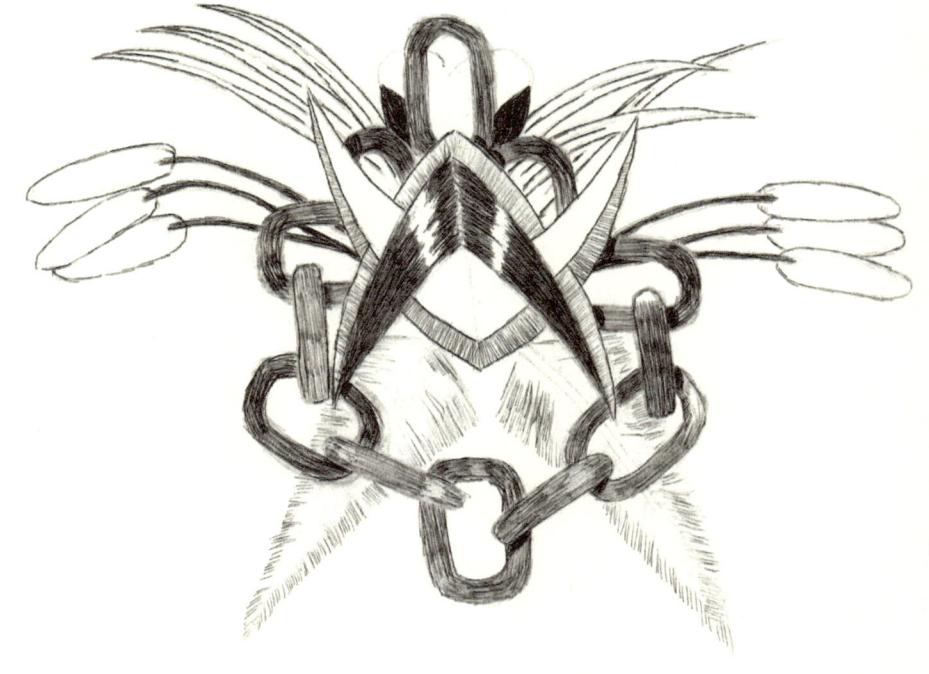

Unlikely Warrior

Stop

It is funny, when I stop, they start.
I stop wanting their friendship, they discover I am alive.
I stop wanting their approval; they see me in a new light.
I stop caring if they like me, at me they begin to smile.
I learn to value my own space, they want to come in and sit down.
Why do I have to stop before they will start?
Does not caring make me more like them?
Does not caring make me make me fit in?
To be uncaring, disdainful and rude, are these characteristics socially
acceptable views?
Why must I become those I dislike in order to survive?
Is it worth it? Is it wise?

Strain

Believe she does finally,
the smile, broad upon her face.
Her eyes dance with the knowledge.
Her heart sings with the phrase.
A weight is lifted from her.
A new person is exposed.
Fragile, beautiful,
but not vulnerable anymore.
The living strain,
a part of the past.
The lust for life consumes her at last.
The pain isn't there.
Now she realizes,
The strain was never due her.
Eyes open
Soul not guarded
It isn't afraid to soar.
No doors closed, in darkness,
I'll sit never anymore.
All this because of five little words, I love you forever more.

They Say

Racism is a thing of the past, they say.
Call one prejudice and they laugh and say your view is a foolish crush.
If you want to succeed you can, they say.
But welfare got you lazy and full, so you don't try, they say.
I watch the news, they say.
I see blacks committing crimes day and night.
You all are a drag on society, they say.
If you are going to be a criminal, you should operate the same as the mafia.
They just kill people who deserved to be killed, they say.
They don' mess with innocent folks.
And the drugs, you should keep the dealing on the down low, like we do in
our neighborhoods, they say.
Hell, police have been driving right by crack houses in our hoods for years.
But we got it on the down low so they don't know, they say.
And we have our drug use under control.
You blacks, Mexicans, Chinese and Indians don't know how to use drugs.
You all don't have self-control, they say.

Tired

As a kid I don't remember being so tired.
When did this happen?
Why didn't I notice?
Why did this occur?
What to do about it I hesitate to ask.
You see, a soul searching answer is required.
And that is too much work for a man already tired
I work hard on the job.
I have no energy left for me.
Is that the problem or a symptom?
I am too confused to see.
Did I take the easy road where I neglect my own metal health?
Did I take the easy rather than fully exploring myself?
Is conforming where the problem lay?
Did it take my ego away?
Did conformity choose my fate?
Put me in a vegetative state?

Tower Pride

Sky powder blue, home to puffs of wispy clouds, drift slowly and carelessly upon lazy currents of air.
The city below is not of them aware.
Its eyes are turned in upon its self-important self.
The task of getting the inhabitants safely through rush hour is at hand.
And the city concentrates solely on that effort.
The highways are at work while the buildings, tall and proud of their work day role, take a well-deserved rest once the two legs are disgorged.
With interest they watch the flight of those they protect from wind, rain and snow.

The single minded fleeing mass, throw no backward glances at their work day homes. They cast them out of their mines and keep their eyes straight on to their personal habitats.

Horns honk angrily and brakes squeal impatiently at drivers whom minds dare stray from the job of getting home.
Young energetic roadsters cut with malice, perilously close in front of more cautious road weary veterans.
The veterans seem to take the antics in stride and continue undaunted on their path.

As rush hour whines down, the city smiles because all in all it handled the press of rushing metal rather smoothly and well.

Evening arrives. The city darkens and takes on a different mood.
Gone is the sense of urgency the production day hours bore.
Under a content moon, the mood is moderate and easy.
Dwellers venture out at a leisurely pace.
On the road in their gleaming stamps of metal some are even courteous now.

But all is not well because the office towers are envious of smaller and more festive brethren.
They resent that these leisure centers receive the gift of laughter and the warmth of happy smiles.
Why if it were not for the office towers the laugh centers would rot away because no one would have money to spend.
With that thought the office towers stand a little straighter.
They are the back bone of the city.
They have seen many frivolous laugh centers come and go.
Laugh center didn't have the staying power of the towers.
But still the towers can't help feeling a bit jealous because all too often laughter doing the work day was sometimes forced and most times short lived.

The old time towers did not care one way or the other.
To them it did not matter what the self-absorbed two legs thought or did.
Years of being used and abused made some old timers dream of a day when no two legs would set foot inside them again.
It was a foolish wish. This they knew.
For without the two legs their days would be few.

What did I do?

What did I do, to make you so mad?
Don't tell me you aren't.
I can see the veins in your head.
Talked about you behind your back?
That isn't me.
Lied on you, cheated?
I could never be so elitist.
Think I'm better than you?
I don't go that route.
Always in your face?
You been smoking without a doubt.
Just pissed you off in general?
That really narrows it down.
I tell you what.
I'll just see you around.

www.ingramcontent.com/pod-product-compliance
Lightning Source LLC
Chambersburg PA
CBHW022125170526
45157CB00004B/1757